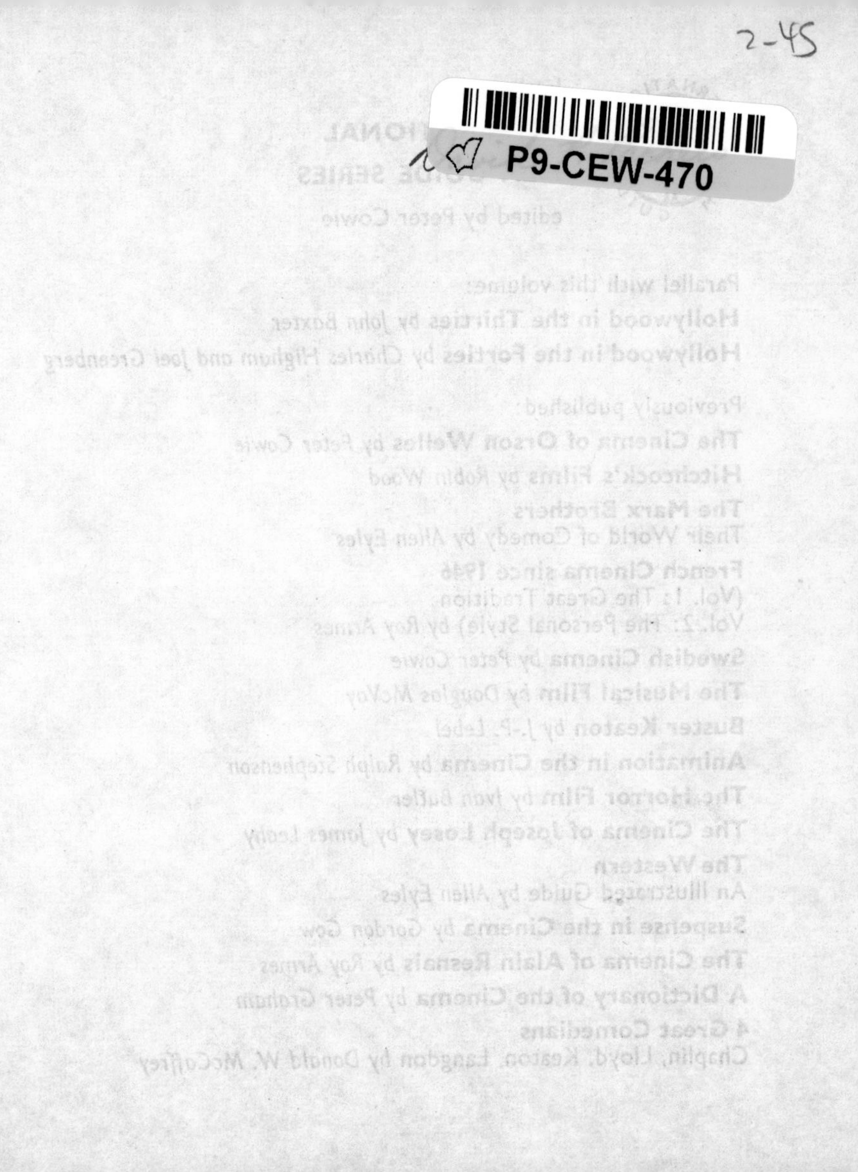
2-45
P9-CEW-470

In the same

INTERNATIONAL

FILM GUIDE SERIES

edited by Peter Cowie

Parallel with this volume:

Hollywood in the Thirties *by John Baxter*

Hollywood in the Forties *by Charles Higham and Joel Greenberg*

Previously published:

The Cinema of Orson Welles *by Peter Cowie*

Hitchcock's Films *by Robin Wood*

The Marx Brothers
Their World of Comedy *by Allen Eyles*

French Cinema since 1946
(Vol. 1: The Great Tradition
Vol. 2: The Personal Style) *by Roy Armes*

Swedish Cinema *by Peter Cowie*

The Musical Film *by Douglas McVay*

Buster Keaton *by J.-P. Lebel*

Animation in the Cinema *by Ralph Stephenson*

The Horror Film *by Ivan Butler*

The Cinema of Joseph Losey *by James Leahy*

The Western
An Illustrated Guide *by Allen Eyles*

Suspense in the Cinema *by Gordon Gow*

The Cinema of Alain Resnais *by Roy Armes*

A Dictionary of the Cinema *by Peter Graham*

4 Great Comedians
Chaplin, Lloyd, Keaton, Langdon *by Donald W. McCaffrey*

HOLLYWOOD IN THE TWENTIES

by

DAVID ROBINSON

★ ★ ★

A. ZWEMMER LIMITED, LONDON
A. S. BARNES & CO., NEW YORK

Front Cover: Clara Bow.

Back Cover: (Twenties) Rudolph Valentino practises the tango; (Thirties) Spencer Tracy in *Twenty Thousand Years in Sing Sing*; (Forties) Joan Crawford in *Mildred Pierce*.

FIRST PUBLISHED 1968

Copyright © 1968 by David Robinson

This edition prepared by The Tantivy Press
in association with A. Zwemmer Ltd.
and A. S. Barnes & Co. Inc.
Library of Congress Catalog Card No. 68-24002
Printed in England by Page & Thomas Ltd., Chesham

Contents

"Oh — I am very youthful, thank God — and rather beautiful, thank God — and happy, thank God, thank God."

Scott Fitzgerald: *This Side of Paradise*

"The United States is the only nation in history to have passed from barbarism to decadence without the usual interval of civilisation."

Clemenceau

Introduction

IT IS a dangerous — and perhaps ultimately doomed — undertaking to compress into a book of this length the story of a cinema as prolific and rich as Hollywood in the decade or so between the end of the First World War and the general introduction of talking pictures. All that is really possible is a bird's eye view of things; and my concern has been to show the films and film-makers of this period both in their relationship to the industry and to the general background of American life and culture in the extraordinary epoch which separated the Armistice from the Wall Street Crash. The sixty or seventy film-makers whose careers are treated in greater or less detail are those whom I feel are most significant or at least most representative in their period. Inevitably other judgements will see partialities and omissions in my selection.

The special difficulty in dealing with a period as remote as this now is, is that such a small proportion of the total output has survived for critical appraisal. So much of film history is composed, consequently, of received opinion; and received opinion is rarely better than misleading. Every time a "lost" film is rediscovered you learn again how irrelevant to our own tastes and values are the judgements of earlier periods. However cautiously you accept the views of contemporary or intervening critics, whatever allowances you make for idiosyncracies of taste and changes of time, every second-hand assessment is likely to be meaningless. Lewis Jacobs devoted three lines to Buster Keaton, for example, in his *Rise of the American Film.* Paul Rotha's *Film Till Now* did him more honour with one paragraph and a half dozen passing mentions. Neither approach bears much relation to present-day evaluation of the comedian.

The difficulty becomes acute when you are dealing with a director like James Cruze, in whose case primary material is practically non-existent. To form any sort of view you must weigh the evidence of contemporary reviewers in *The Bioscope* and *Variety*, the opinions of Rotha and Jacobs; and you still know that you are going to arrive at an untrustworthy answer to the questions which we, in the late Sixties, are asking. All I can claim is that I have worked as far as possible from first-hand viewing in arriving at critical assessments; and that in any case the emphasis of this study is factual rather than critical.

The bibliography of the period is far too large to detail. I must acknowledge a continuing debt to Rotha and Jacobs; and to Gertrude Jobes's *Motion Picture Empire*; to the files of *Bioscope*, *Kinematograph Weekly*, *Variety*, *Picturegoer*, *Films in Review*, *Sight and Sound*; to the *Enciclopedia dello Spettacolo*; and to innumerable memoirs of the period. For the social and political background of the Twenties I have referred to Arthur M. Schlesinger Jr.'s *The Age of Roosevelt: The Crisis of the Old Order*, Frederick Lewis Allen's *Only Yesterday*, Lloyd Morris's *Not So Long Ago*, Isabel Leighton's *The Aspirin Age* and the *LIFE History of the United States*. Primarily of course I must acknowledge the collections of the National Film Archive.

For personal help I am especially grateful to Miss Brenda Davies, Head of the Information Department of the British Film Institute, and Gillian Hartnoll, Book Librarian of the National Film Archive, who has made many very valuable suggestions; and to Kevin Brownlow, the only authority who has a true grasp of the techniques as well as the art and history of the silent cinema, and whose patience in answering silly questions is astonishing.

1. The Nation

FOUR DECADES after the introduction of talking pictures, there are grave difficulties in the appreciation of the films of America's post-war decade. We are dealing, first of all, with a dead art: the silent cinema developed expressive means that were self-sufficient, but which are now unfamiliar and remote. To add to our problems, we generally see these films in duped and decayed and corrupted copies, which can recall little of their original brightness and impact. And we see so few of them, in isolation from each other and from the context in which they first appeared and were first seen. They can only profitably be discussed in relation to, and in the terms of the society which produced them and for whose pleasure they were produced.

Perhaps at no time in their history — not even in 1776 or the Civil War — did the American people undergo such profound changes in their ways of life and thought as in the years that began with the Armistice and ended with the Stock Market crash. These years covered just over a decade. When they began the horse and buggy still lingered. They ended to the roar of cars and aeroplanes. The decade began, significantly, with *Broken Blossoms* and *Pollyanna*, and ended with *The Crowd* and *The Wedding March*. It was an era in which, wrote Scott Fitzgerald, "America was going on the greatest, gaudiest spree in history."

Fitzgerald wrote also, "It was characteristic of the Jazz Age that it had no interest in politics at all." Yet the administrations which guided America through these years impose their own strongly defined patterns upon the times. As the war ended, Woodrow Wilson had been in office for five years. At the moment in December 1918 that he went to the Paris Peace Conference, he enjoyed a universal esteem and affection such as few politicians have ever known. He was cheered by crowds in France, Italy and England as enthusiastically as by the Americans who saw him off on the "George Washington".

His triumph was brief. His uncompromising idealism had chimed with the mood of a nation and a world at war. But peace brought a change of outlook. Both in Paris and at home there was reaction: the prevailing mood shifted from the co-operative optimism of war to a general feeling of fear and hate and isolation. The majority of the representatives at the conference table were dedicated to revenge upon Germany — making the pips squeak — and territorial advantage to their own countries. Wilson returned to America in June 1919, perhaps more conscious of how his hopes for a noble settlement had been compromised, than how much worse it would have been without his wise and stubborn counsels. Back home he met violent criticism of the Treaty of Versailles. Every immigrant community found some objection to it, while the people at large had retreated from Wilsonian idealism to a mixture of isolationist apathy and vindictive Hun-hating. The Committee on Foreign Relations, far from ratifying the treaty, voted amendment after amendment.

Wilson, in desperation, embarked on a marathon speaking tour throughout the West, hoping to win back the support of the people. Already exhausted with overwork, he suffered a severe stroke. Yet for seventeen more months he remained in office, frail, sick, confined to the White House, rarely communicating directly with the outside world, rejecting his closest friends and supporters. Mrs. Wilson was spoken of as a regent, and nicknamed the first woman president of the United States. In these strange times the executive of the United States seemed to have come to a halt. Meanwhile the Treaty for which Wilson had sacrificed his person was defeated.

Ironically, it was during the administration of Wilson, the great liberal idealist, that America underwent the first of the great "Red Scares" that were to leave their scars upon the nation's psychology throughout the twentieth century. This first post-war scare assumed alarming proportions. Ordinary Americans were disturbed by the spectacle of what was taking place in Russia, and by industrial unrest and strikes at home; and their apprehensions were played on by the American business man, who saw his profits threatened by organisation of labour. Radical political activity was blamed for a number of bomb scares in 1919: the majority of thirty-six bombs sent through the post were thwarted for the rather engaging reason that the senders had inadequately franked them. One of a further series of bombs damaged the home of the Attorney-General, Palmer. In retaliation, defenders of law, order and the American way of life — often reinforced by high-spirited and undirected ex-servicemen — smashed up Socialist meetings and premises, inflicting injury and in some cases loss of life. (Scott Fitzgerald describes one such incident in his horrifying little story, *May Day*.)

The Red scare reached a peak of hysteria in the monstrous Palmer Raids, in which some 6,000 suspected Communists were rounded up, and in many cases deported, while people who visited them in prison were quite liable to be themselves arrested. Intolerance, masquerading as patriotism, grew in those years until a writer in *Harpers* in 1922 could say, "America is no longer a free country, in the old sense . . . everywhere, on every hand, free speech is choked off in one direction or another." All-American solidarity led to persecution of other minorities apart from socialists: racial hatred reached unprecedented virulence in the early Twenties, at a time when coloured Americans, returning from the war, felt a new consciousness of equality (cf. G. B. Seitz's film version of *The Vanishing American*). 1919 and 1920 saw fatal colour riots in Chicago and Tulsa.

Jews, equally, were identified with the Bolsheviks and other un-American elements. Henry Ford's anti-Jewish propaganda, which later won him a high award from Hitler, was not the isolated whim of a rich man. Even the Catholic church was blackened with charges of un-Americanism. It was this mood which encouraged the growth of the Ku Klux Klan, which increased from a few hundred members at the end of the war to more than four million in the mid-Twenties; for the Klan offered to frightened, vicious and often poor men the opportunity to work behind masks and to perpetrate all kinds of satisfying cruelties and horrors.

The worst of the scare was over shortly after the start of the Twenties, when Harding's election and other sensations distracted the public's attention; but the Red Scare has proved an enduring element of fear, an indelible fact of American life.

* * *

The genial, small-town, eminently accessible President Warren Gamaliel Harding with his essential realism, and his narrow policy of political isolation, could hardly have provided a more dramatic contrast to Wilson's high-minded and visionary sermons on duty. The Republican elders nominated him as a man they could control, and a Republican senator described him as "the best of the second-raters", though in after years *Life* amended this: "Harding proved in fact one of the worst of the second-raters." Opposed by another nonentity, Governor James Cox, Harding was swept to office by a clear majority.

William Gibbs McAdoo said that Harding's oratory gave the impression "of an army of pompous phrases moving over the landscape in search of an idea. Sometimes these meandering words would actually capture a straggling thought and bear it triumphantly, a prisoner in their midst, until it died of servitude and overwork." On one occasion, however, his poor command of language and still weaker hold on notions triumphed, to produce the term "normalcy", which seemed to reflect the aspirations and the character of a whole brief era of American history. "The nation was spiritually tired. Wearied by the excitements of war and the nervous tension of the Big Red Scare, they hoped for quiet and healing. Sick of Wilson and his talk of America's duty to humanity, callous to political idealism, they hoped for a chance to pursue their private affairs without governmental interference and to forget about public affairs. There might be no such word in the dictionary as normalcy, but normalcy was what they wanted." (F. L. Allen).

The easy air of the Harding administration suited the times; and somehow the massive public corruption also reflected the public mood — to the extent that when the skeletons all rattled out of the Harding wardrobe, people were not so outraged by the grafters as by those who had exposed them. Harding delighted America with his warmth and neighbourliness, even if the warmth were disproportionately radiated in the direction of business America. Neighbourliness was his undoing. He brought to Washington and high office old cronies from his years in small-town Ohio. At first eyebrows were raised only at the extreme informality of social life at the White House and the President's passion for poker and liquor. Then it was noted that a surprising number of pardons was being granted to criminals who were notorious but also rich. Harding's brother-in-law was superintendent of Federal Prisons. In 1922 one of Harding's best friends, Charles R. Forbes, was found to be using his post as Director of the Veterans' Bureau for million-dollar graft. Two sinister suicides and increasingly ugly rumours followed. In July 1923 the President left for Alaska for the good of his health, and arrived back dead. Dreadful rumours circulated and were not calmed by the official report that Harding's illness had begun with ptomaine poisoning from crab meat served on the Presidential boat, since the boat's stores carried no crab meat. There were even those who said and wrote that the ambitious Mrs. Harding had murdered her husband, either out of jealousy or to save him from the scandal that was inevitable.

For only after the President's death did the worst secrets emerge — the great oil lease scandals and the corruption of Albert Fall; the sordid revelations of Nan Britton, Harding's mistress, who claimed that her illegitimate child had been conceived in the Senate Office Building; the graft of the Alien Property Custodian's Office; massive protection pay-offs received from prohibition gangsters. "The Harding adminstration was responsible in its short two years," wrote Frederick Lewis Allen, "for more concentrated robbery and rascality than any other in the whole history of the Federal Government." "Harding was not a bad man," said Alice Roosevelt Longworth, "He was just a slob."

* * *

Harding's successor, another complete contrast, deserves our gratitude because in his obscure small-town youth he had given the young Mack Sennett a terse letter of recommendation to the star comedienne Marie Dressler. The subsequent meeting got Sennett nowhere, but it fired his ambitions to work in show business. Dry, severe, Calvin Coolidge was as cold and remote as Harding had been gregarious. In his limited way he was incorruptible. His policies, domestic and foreign, were conservative and unheroic. His prose and oratory were commonplace and turgid, but correct. But just like Harding he managed to sum up his era and its aspirations with perfect accuracy. "The chief business of the American people is business." "This is a business country; it wants a business government." "The man who builds a factory builds a temple . . . the man who works there worships there."

This comparison of business and religion was by no means unusual in the mid-Twenties. A best-seller of 1925-6, "The Man Nobody Knows", by Bruce Barton, who was later religious adviser on DeMille's *King of Kings*, solemnly traced the parallels between Christianity and Big Business, identifying Jesus in terms of a modern tycoon. Coolidge was more than sympathetic to American Business, which by 1923 had made a startling recovery from the depression of two years earlier. "Coolidge prosperity" was to increase and last for seven giddy years. The farmers stood outside the general boom, as did certain other industries, including coal and cotton; but most of America wondered and rejoiced at its new prosperity and produced and consumed and spent. Between 1920 and 1929 industrial production increased almost 50% and the national income grew from 79.1 billion dollars to almost 88 billion.

There were a number of causes for prosperity — none of them especially to the personal credit of Calvin Coolidge. America had gained great mercantile advantage from the war, which she was now able to follow up with sheer resources and with the Fordist streamlining of mass production. Investment in industry during these years (as 1930 was so disastrously to prove) was immense. And America, stimulated by salesmanship and advertising — activities which had become patriotic duty — had learned to consume as no people had ever consumed before. Americans bought houses, automobiles, household appliances, radios, washing machines, new foods and refrigerators to keep them in. The frenzy of consumption is constantly reflected in films of the period with their emphasis on clothes and cars and decoration, though never more than in the orgiastic destruction of consumer goods that characterises the Sennett comedies.

* * *

Herbert Hoover was swept into office by a landslide at the peak of the boom. He had campaigned largely on the Republican achievement of abolishing poverty throughout the States; and when he was elected, the new slogan of American business was "four more years of prosperity." In his election campaign he had said, "We in America today are nearer to the final triumph over poverty than ever before in the history of the land . . . Given a chance to go forward with the policies of the last eight years, we shall soon with the help of God be in sight of the day when poverty will be banished from this nation." Perhaps God withheld His help: this was a mere fifteen months before the great crash.

Speculation had entered America's blood during the Coolidge years. The great bull market came from a mass desire to gamble on prosperity. 1928-9 saw an unprecedented stock-buying spree. Despite an occasional earth-tremor on the market, everyone bought and stocks rose and rose. Scott Fitzgerald, on a trip to New York in 1929, found that his barber had retired after making half a million on the market. In 1928 alone Montgomery Ward stocks went up from 117 to 440 and R.C.A. from 85 to 420.

Nobody has been quite able to explain the causes of the great crash of 1929. A weak banking system, shaky corporate organisation, an unfavourable international balance of trade, above all maldistribution of income, restricting the consumption power of the mass of Americans and exaggerating the power to affect the economy of that 5% of the population which, in 1929, received one third of all personal income were some factors. Whatever the causes, the crash came. Despite brave efforts by the bankers to bolster the market, the crisis began on Black Thursday, October 24th, 1929. By mid-November, paper fortunes worth thirty billion dollars had been wiped out on the New York Stock Market. An era had ended.

★ ★ ★

The Twenties was an age of revolution in communications. American life was transformed in varying degrees and varying ways by the effects of cars, radio, advertising and the cinema. The first cars had appeared on American roads in the 1890s and Ford had produced his first T model in 1908. But it was in the Twenties that the full effects of his revolution in industrial methods and the effects of motorisation upon American civilisation began really to be felt.

Between 1918 and 1929 the national registration of motor vehicles rose from less than six million to more than twenty-three million; while the roads of America progressed from the haphazard mud-track explorations of the nineteenth century to a complex modern highway system that covered the entire area of the United States. In 1909 there were only 725 miles of paved rural roads; twenty years later there were more than 100,000. The whole aspect of the country was changed. Buster Keaton's *Our Hospitality* was shot in 1923 in the Lake Tahoe and Truckee Valley region, three hundred miles north of Hollywood and then in all its wild, unspoiled splendour. Almost before the arrival of talking pictures, it would be invaded by motels and filling stations and tourist camps.

It was not only the rural landscape that was changed by the automobile. Cities spread out along the new roads, and new communities and community centres grew up. People's marketing habits changed. America, generally, grew smaller. Rural communities were no longer isolated, no longer tied to one church, the village school and to the uncertain attentions of the village doctor. The horse and buggy peace of *Tol'able David* vanished before the encroachment of urban ways and standardised metropolitan values. The traffic jam became an established feature of rural as of urban life.

Patterns of leisure changed: camping, golf, touring, the pursuit of the countryside enjoyed new vogues. Static holidays declined — and with them the old holiday centres — as America took to wheels. Cars contributed to the general break-up of social and family habits that was characteristic of the period. The car was a new expression of independence for the young and offered new opportunities of promiscuity to all, for it was said that America now made love in automobiles. Cars were a delight to censorious magistrates, who complained that one third of all sex crimes were committed in automobiles.

The car affected life in more sombre ways. Road accidents increased:

by 1940 they would account for one million injured people every year, and 40,000 deaths. New crimes were introduced — the accident insurance racket, and highway robbery committed by thieves posing as hitch-hikers. And of course the motor car became the principal tool of the gangsters; so that the term "to be taken for a ride" lost all the sunny meaning of pre-prohibition days.

The automobile industry became crucial to American business. In the course of the decade Americans spent something like thirty billion dollars on cars. What was good for General Motors . . . men like William Crapo Durant and Henry Ford were giants. Ford in particular became an archetypal, Horatio Alger folk hero: the Michigan farmboy, the impoverished inventor, the small-town tinkerer who became a multi-millionaire. He gave America Barney Oldfield and the Tin Lizzie. He hallowed big business: "There is something sacred about big business which provides a living for hundreds and thousands of families." He helped establish that confidence in business which is the key to American politics to this day. He created modern production-line methods, so that by 1922 he could boast that there remained no single hand operation at his Highland Park factory. In other respects too he was a pioneer. At the Ford factory, in the pre-war period, twentieth century mass production existed alongside nineteenth century ideas of sweated labour. In 1914 Ford reacted to growing labour problems by announcing a "profit-sharing plan" which would double the standard day's price for common labour to five dollars. Though nobody was under any illusion about Ford's motives, we can date from this moment a whole modern conception of industrial employment and industrial paternalism which was to have a world-wide influence. Ford's Highland Park factory was a social experiment as well as an industrial miracle; even though Ford in later years was to denounce paternalism in industry.

He was always capricious and unpredictable. For years throughout the Twenties and Thirties he opposed labour organisation in his factories, by means of a large and notorious strong-arm force. Yet when finally his methods were exposed, Ford made a complete *volte face* and not only admitted the unions, but actually co-operated to assist them in their organisation and the collection of dues.

Despite his attacks on the Jews, and the war-time debacle of his celebrated "Peace Ship", Ford retained the affection and reverence of the American people. Perhaps the very meanness and narrowness of his views found some echo in the general public, who saw in him the champion of free enterprise, the living proof of American opportunity and the triumph of big business. Always a strange figure, Ford, the architect of the twentieth century industrial revolution, remained a man of the nineteenth century in his instincts and intelligence; and it is even a little pathetic that in later years he devoted vast sums in a hopeless attempt to buy back the world of his boyhood, dedicating himself to the revival of early American folk music and dance, and building at Greenfield Village a place where no cars ran.

The complex figure of Ford is reflected in its many facets in a hundred characterisations of tycoons in Twenties films. And the motor car is all pervasive in the movies of these times — whether crashing, collapsing or chasing up walls in the Keystone comedy, or roaring to murder and revenge in gangster films, or elegantly carrying dancing mothers and dancing daughters, or providing the erotic arena for the young people of the Jazz Age.

This was also the age of radio. Radio had developed with astonishing speed since Wilson broadcast the fourteen points to the world by means of wireless in January 1918, and Dr. Frank Conrad first began regular transmissions from a radio station built over his garage in Pittsburgh in the spring of 1920. By the end of 1922 there were 220 stations on the air, and manufacturers of receivers were hard pressed to keep up with the demand. Announcers, like early movie stars, were at first anonymous; but as the Twenties went on radio personalities achieved immense popularity. The pattern of commercial broadcasting was established late in 1922 when the American Teleprinter and Telegraph Company transmitted a commercial for a new co-operative apartment house.

Politically and culturally, radio (like the cinema) transformed

America, unifying the nation, breaking through geographical and class barriers to create a vast, cohesive unit. The contrast between the whistle-stop tour which broke President Wilson as he vainly tried to appeal to the American people in 1918 and the effectiveness of Roosevelt's fireside talks at the start of the Thirties, is self-explanatory.

At the same time, and considerably helped by radio, advertising became a key motive force in the consumer society. Articles by Jesse Ransford Sprague in *Harpers* revealed the dreadful pressure that was applied to salesmen to make them pass on the pressure to their customers. The Twenties developed practically all the modern techniques of advertising and salesmanship. Before the war advertisers had sold their goods by means of simple information. By the Twenties contemporary methods of advertising applied a kind of social and sexual blackmail.

★ ★ ★

Americans in the Twenties were fascinated (and the fascination is nowhere more clearly reflected than in the movies of the time) with the New Morality. The immediate post-war mood was shot through with a reckless desire to make up for the deprivations and disappointments of the war years. The boys returned from Europe with a new kind of maturity and independence acquired from exposure to European manners and European standards. Some of the girls, too, had seen the independence of service as nurses and war workers; all of them experienced emancipation in several forms. Not only had women won the suffrage in 1920, but a large-scale revolution in domestic life gave them a different kind of independence. Demanding Victorian ideals of domesticity were swept away; smaller houses and the gospel of labour-saving offered a new freedom. "Solitary dishing isn't enough to satisfy me — or many other women," says Carol Kennicott, the heroine of *Main Street*; "We're going to chuck it. We're going to wash 'em by machinery, and come out and play with you men in the offices and clubs and politics you've cleverly kept for yourselves! Oh, we're hopeless, we dissatisfied women!" She voiced the sentiments of many married women — as well as single ones — who made the revolt and went out to work.

The Younger Generation, as it was called, was in violent reaction against its elders. It had found, said Scott Fitzgerald, "All gods dead, all wars fought, all faiths in man shaken." "Mother, it's done," says a young lady in *This Side of Paradise*; "you can't run everything the way you did — in the Nineties"; and the hero of the same novel writes:

Victorians, Victorians, who never learned to weep,
Who sowed the bitter harvest that your children go to reap.

Girls frankly smoked, drank, petted, used make-up, rolled their stockings, cut their hair, abandoned corsets and petticoats and wore skirts that got shorter every season, rising by a clear 9 in. between 1919 and 1927. (These trends resulted in striking industrial reactions: the changing habits of American women produced booms in the cigarette, cosmetic and rayon industries, though other textile industries suffered seriously by the reduction of a woman's clothing to barely one third of its pre-war yardage, while corset-manufacturers experienced an almost fatal slump.)

Bad manners and drinking too much were in order in these stridently assertive times. Cecilia Connage thought her sister "average — smokes sometimes, drinks punch, frequently kissed — Oh, yes — common knowledge — one of the effects of the war you know." "None of the Victorian mothers — and most of the mothers were Victorian — had any idea how casually their daughters were accustomed to be kissed. '*Servant*-girls are that way,' says Mrs. Huston-Carmelite to her popular daughter. 'They are kissed first and proposed to afterwards . . . .'"

"Amory saw girls doing things that even in his memory would have been impossible, eating three-o'clock, after-dance suppers in impossible cafés, talking of every side of life with an air half of earnestness, half of mockery, yet with a furtive excitement that Amory considered stood for real moral let-down. But he never realised how wide-spread it was until he saw the cities between New York and Chicago as one vast juvenile intrigue."

This Side of Paradise was for many people the first, shocking intimation of the new morality — the petting parties, the automobile romances and all. The cinema would provide other, no less vivid instances. The older generation inevitably followed the example of the younger; Dancing Mothers followed on the high heels of Dancing Daughters.

The extent of pre- and extra-marital experience remains an intriguing mystery. Freud, interpreted mistily at second and third hand, seemed a licence for sexual freedom, and the Twenties astonished themselves with their abandoning of inhibitions of every sort. The mood of the times produced a vogue in sexy literature and sexy films. Subjects that were unmentionable before the war became almost boring as topics of conversation after it. Practically no subject was now taboo, as some of the most successful plays of the years demonstrated.

It would of course be a mistake to imagine all America undergoing the same revolution. The Victorian outlook of Gopher Prairie survived after reaction and disillusion had set in, as it still survives to a degree today. But the watchword was "modern"; and America had its own strong image of its present; and tried to live up to it.

★ ★ ★

The Eighteenth Amendment — and Prohibition — was accepted with surprising ease. There was little organised opposition and no one seemed to have any conception of what would be its outcome. The Eighteenth Amendment had been swept along on the wave of war-time idealism. The drying-out of America in 1920 coincided with the birth of the Roaring Twenties, an age yearning for relaxation of every code. Small wonder that from the very first it proved practically impossible to enforce the Volstead Act to the smallest degree. With Harding dispensing hard liquor in the White House itself, and with cocktail parties the current vogue and the speakeasies flourishing as nightspots with the extra spice of criminality to recommend them, those whose task was to enforce the Act found little support in public opinion. Evasion — by smuggling, by diversion of legitimate medical or industrial alcohol supplies; above all by illicit brewing and distilling — reached massive proportions.

The huge profits waiting for the prohibition racketeer was a root cause of that unparalleled decade of gangsterism and gang warfare which began, properly speaking, around 1920, when Johnny Torrio engaged Al Capone as his lieutenant, and which reached its climax in 1929 with the St. Valentine's Day killings. Other circumstances, of course, favoured gangsterism at this particular period in American history — the automobile, weapons like the Thompson sub-machine gun which had come into their own during the war; political apathy; the increasing power of the Mafia. The gangsters did not confine themselves to liquor activities alone: their incomes were augmented by gambling enterprises, vice and resorts of pleasure, and by some of the cruellest protection rackets ever devised. (In the Thirties, these protection rackets, in relation to labour organisation, would be applied to the cinema itself.)

★ ★ ★

A significant phenomenon of the age was the development of the tabloid newspapers. (How useful their dramatic front pages and terse headlines were to prove to film-makers!) *The New York Daily News* began publication in the summer of 1919; by 1920 its circulation was over one and a quarter million. Taken together with the rise of big circulation national magazines, the publicity agent and broadcasting, the tabloids, with their emphasis on crime and sex and sport and every novel excitement, contributed much to the image of the Twenties as the age of ballyhoo and passing crazes among which were Mahjong, Emile Coué, Tut-Ank-Amen, Bathing Beauties, crossword puzzle books (the making of Simon and Schuster), the Prince of Wales, Aimée MacPherson and Billy Sunday, Marathon Dancing and Flagpole Squatting. Cash-and-Carry Piles' Bunion Derby found an echo in Harry Langdon's *Tramp*, *Tramp*, *Tramp*. It was an age of wacky hit-songs, though none achieved greater success than "Yes, we have no Bananas", which inspired a "Zit's Comedy" in 1923. It was an age of sensational crime:

the Elwell Case, the Hall-Mills murders; the Snyder Gray trial; Leopold and Loeb, and, on a lighter level, the Daddy Browning divorce case. The Sacco and Vanzetti case wound on from 1920 to 1927, uniting liberal thought against a monstrous official condoning of injustice.

Two events of these years were to provide substantial themes for motion pictures, long after the end of the silent era. A young man named Floyd Collins became front-page news in February 1925, when he was trapped in an underground cave where he died, amidst the glare of arc-lights and publicity, eighteen days later. Collins was the original of Billy Wilder's *The Big Carnival* (*Ace in the Hole*). The Dayton Monkey Trial, in which a school teacher was charged with the offence of teaching the theory of evolution (and which later provided the subject for the film *Inherit the Wind*) attracted nation-wide attention later the same year. It was a significant confrontation of the old religion and the new scepticism, within the churches, of the Fundamentalists and the Modernists, the past and the present.

The Twenties were years of great sport and sportsmen. There had never been a bigger fight than the Dempsey-Carpentier match of 1921; but it was only the first of many million-dollar matches which culminated in the two Dempsey-Tunney fights of 1926-27. As Keaton's films in particular reflect, it was a period of intense enthusiasm for baseball and racing and golf and college football. Bobby Jones and Walter Hagen were the most notable of two million golfing Americans. Baseball gates soared; and Babe Ruth was a national hero. Red Grange was the football star of his age. William Tilden won seven American Amateur Tennis Championships. Gertrude Ederle was the first woman to swim the Channel.

In all the ballyhoo years however, nothing was quite so remarkable as the adulation of Lindbergh, after his frankly stunt flight of May 1927. Frederick Lewis Allen, a shrewd observer of American sentiment in these years summed it up: "A disillusioned nation fed on cheap heroics and scandal and crime was revolting against the low estimate of human nature which it had allowed itself to entertain. For years the American people had been spiritually starved. . . . Something that people needed, if they were to live at peace with themselves and with the world, was missing from their lives. And all at once Lindbergh provided it. Romance, chivalry, self-dedication — here they were, embodied in a modern Galahad for a generation which had forsworn Galahads."

★ ★ ★

For the American ideals of the Harding and Coolidge eras had not gone unquestioned. Not all Americans in the Twenties were dedicated to the religion of big business, worship of Tunney, Tilden and Red Grange, committed to the New Morality, wedded to cars and radios, enslaved by advertising. Not all were reading Elinor Glyn, Confession Magazines, Bruce Barton or *The Sheik*. Not all were like those inhabitants of Gopher Prairie, "a savourless people, gulping tasteless food, and sitting afterwards, coatless and thoughtless, in rocking chairs prickly with inane decorations, listening to mechanical music, saying mechanical things about the excellence of Ford automobiles, and viewing themselves as the greatest race in the world." There were the others, the rebels like the authors whom Carol Kennicott read, and who were "most of them frightfully annoyed by the Vida Sherwins. They were young American sociologists, young English realists, Russian horrorists; Anatole France, Rolland, Nexo, Wells, Shaw, Key, Edgar Lee Masters, Theodore Dreiser, Sherwood Anderson, Henry Mencken, and all the other subversive philosophers and artists whom women were consulting everywhere in batik-curtained studios in New York, in Kansas farm-houses, San Francisco drawing rooms, Alabama schools for negroes." The young dissenters found leadership in the American Mercury, in which H. L. Mencken's revolt against the business culture led him to an anarchic repudiation of the very principles of democracy. Irving Babbitt likewise questioned the workings of American society. Sinclair Lewis attacked small-town philistinism and self-satisfaction in *Main Street* and *Babbitt* and cheap-jack religion in *Elmer Gantry*. Dreiser, Anderson *et al* encouraged scepticism about the accepted values of American orthodoxy. The intellectuals were in the vanguard of the disillusion — with sex, science and freedom alike — which began to set in in the last quarter of the Twenties, when the rapture of the first post-war sense of emancipation had worn thin, and which found its most precise expression in Joseph Wood Krutch's *The Modern Temper*, published in 1929.

American culture as a whole acquired a new self-confidence as the Twenties progressed. For centuries, Americans had imported their culture from the old world. Now there began to be a consciousness of the worth not only of American writing, but of American music and painting and above all architecture, in which the New World now took the lead. The American theatre, too, moved in these years from the nineteenth century to the twentieth. Despite all fears of the effects of cinema competition, the live theatre flourished. (Between 1926 and 1928 alone twelve new theatres opened in New York.) In 1915 the Theatre Guild and the Neighborhood Players gave their first performances and in the following year the Provincetown Players were founded. This last company presented most of the early plays of O'Neill, whose most influential work appeared in the course of the post-war decade. Sidney Howard, Robert Emmett Sherwood, Maxwell Anderson (whose collaborator on *What Price Glory?*, Lawrence Stallings, became a Hollywood darling), Hatcher Hughes, Elmer Rice — much influenced by the European *avant-garde* — and John Howard Lawson (later one of the most distinguished Hollywood writers) all made their appearance in the Twenties. Their work, and the work of the great designers like Lee Simonson, Norman Bel Geddes and Robert Edmond Jones (who worked with great success in Hollywood), was ultimately to make its influence felt in the film industry.

2. The Industry

BARELY TWENTY YEARS after the first Lumière show in Paris, the cinema had become America's fifth industry. By the time that talking pictures revolutionised Hollywood, the movies had moved up to become the nation's fourth largest industry. This rapid growth was owed more to greed and ambition than to artistic aspiration.

It is interesting to consider the men who were responsible for the industrial development of the movies and who ruled the American cinema in the Twenties. Adolph Zukor was born in Hungary and emigrated to America in 1888, with forty dollars sewn in the lining of his suit. Carl Laemmle came to the States from Germany four years before Zukor and worked for years in menial jobs. William Fox, born in Hungary, was brought to America as a child and before he was seven was helping to support his impoverished family by peddling blacking. Louis B. Mayer, the son of Polish Jews, was born in Minsk and started his life in the new world as a beachcomber and scrap dealer. Sam Goldfish (later Goldwyn) was born in 1884 in Poland, and emigrated at the age of eleven. Harry, Abe, Sam and Jack Warner were the sons of a Polish immigrant cobbler. The eldest boys, Sam and Abe, did all kinds of menial work before they encountered the Edison Kinetoscope while working in an amusement arcade. Marcus Loew sold newspapers until he managed to find a job in the fur trade. Their careers all followed much the same pattern: by the turn of the century each had scraped together a small nest egg which was sufficient to buy a nickelodeon or penny arcade in which they rightly saw a substantial future investment. They were men who knew how to fight for survival; and these were the men who survived the cut-throat industrial wars that characterised the years between 1918 and the coming of sound — the years in which the surviving patterns of the American film industry were established.

On the eve of the First World War, with the final defeat of the great Patents Trust, the organisations which would dominate the industry were beginning to take form. In 1912 Carl Laemmle had established

Universal and spent the succeeding years jockeying for power with his various partners. In 1914 Adolph Zukor had united his own production company, Famous Players, with Jesse Lasky; and formed Paramount Pictures to distribute their combined product. A little later Paramount's capital was raised to ten million dollars. William Fox merged his Box Office Attractions into the Fox Film Company. Marcus Loew, Nicholas and Joseph Schenck and David Bernstein, executives of the Loew vaudeville circuit, established a million dollar picture organisation. In 1915 Richard Rowland and a group of partners who included Louis B. Mayer inaugurated Metro Pictures. Sam Goldfish parted from Zukor to form the Goldwyn Company. Most of the old firms which had been great powers under the Patents Trust — Edison, Kalem, Lubin, Biograph, Thanhouser — dwindled or vanished, though in 1916 Vitagraph, whose history went back to 1897, was recapitalised by B. B. Hampton, the tobacco millionaire, and enjoyed a startling renaissance until it was absorbed by the Warner Brothers ten years later. Triangle had rebuilt its fortunes on *Birth of a Nation* and Charles Chaplin, though it was to collapse — following the departure of Griffith, Ince and Sennett — in 1918.

The war years also had seen the movies move definitively into the age of superlatives. Film moguls thought in millions and played poker for thousand dollar stakes. Productions were Stupendous and Colossal. Star salaries shot up to regal and astronomical sums. Factories were known as studios. Cinema theatres, from being dirty, stuffy converted stores, became palaces.

One characteristic of the pre-war industry had been the film producers' oppressive and at best cavalier treatment of exhibitors — by the imposition of exclusive and block booking systems and every kind of extortion they could legally (or better still, illegally) devise. Matters inevitably improved slightly with the smashing of the Trust; but in April 1917, on the initiative of an exhibitor called Tom Tally, the First National Exhibitors Circuit was established "to demand reasonable, dependable service for $20,000,000 worth of theatres" (Gertrude Jobe: "Motion Picture Empire"). Almost immediately First National went into production. When the company acquired sole distribution rights to Chaplin's films, the rest of the industry was forced to abandon its dictatorial approach and to woo exhibitors with fairer terms and better pictures.

The war itself had produced a temporary boom, which sagged dangerously as a public, at first eager for films about the war, returned to the more mundane tasks which war brought. 1918 saw the industry in straits in which practically all but the major companies — Universal, Metro, Fox, Famous Players-Lasky and Paramount, First National — went to the wall. Of the smaller concerns Warner Brothers alone had a temporary affluence, due to one of the rare successes of 1918, *My Four Years in Germany*, an independently produced screen version of Ambassador Gerard's book, of which they held distribution rights. Their success led them to go into production.

The epidemic of Spanish 'flu in 1918, emptying the cinemas and even taking its toll of executive personnel, was a further disaster. Meanwhile European countries took the opportunity offered by the debilitation of the American film industry to impose embargoes on the importation of American films. Hollywood entered the post-war era as inauspiciously as might have been, with studios inactive, markets reduced, and a backlog of war films which nobody wanted to see.

Yet at the very moment of lowest ebb, when production had come practically to a standstill and theatre owners were putting up their cinemas for sale, the tide turned dramatically. Everyone, it seemed, suddenly wanted to buy theatres — the war's *nouveau riche*, the dispossessed saloon proprietors, put out of business by Prohibition, and, not least, the bankers and financiers. Once the real-estate end of the industry was revived, prosperity seemed to snowball throughout the whole film business. Theatre owners vied with each other in building bigger and grander cinemas, and producers were in business again to supply the reawakened market. Warners built a studio. The Goldwyn Company acquired new capital and took over the former Triangle Studios.

Big new organisations were set up. In 1919 the biggest creative names in the business, artists "too expensive for any single company to maintain on a permanent payroll" — Griffith, Chaplin, Pickford and Fairbanks — organised themselves as United Artists, to distribute the finest independent production. So worried was Zukor, who had relinquished Mary Pickford's services at the height of the depression, that he offered her a quarter of a million dollars to retire from the screen for the next five years! When this ruse failed, Famous Players-Lasky put Mary Miles Minter under contract with the intention of building her into a rival of Little Mary. Shortly after this, a group of directors and producers — Ince, Vidor, Allan Dwan, George Loane Tucker, Sennett, Marshall Neilan, Maurice Tourneur, V. Parker Reade Jr. — formed a similar organisation, which they called Associated Producers. In 1921 this group was merged with First National to become Associated First National.

For some time Wall Street had been intrigued by the large sums of money which the nickels and dimes of millions of Americans contributed to the film industry. The Great Red Scare of the early Twenties was a considerable extra stimulus to this interest. Big Business saw in movies more than a good investment. As "the foremost entertainer and educator of the world's millions" it was a great weapon to combat Bolshevism. The capitalists of America could recognise the opiate of the masses as clearly as Marx or Lenin. Celebrating the virtues of the American way of life and attacking the iniquities of Soviet Russia, the cinema was potentially a good deal more effective than Palmer Raids or breaking up socialist meetings. Wall Street moved in. Famous Players-Lasky capital was upped to twenty million dollars and the bankers and brokers pushed money into every other substantial film concern. William Randolph Hearst established Cosmopolitan Pictures to provide a showcase for the talents of Marion Davies, whom he had first admired as a showgirl in Ziegfeld's chorus line.

"New men from Wall Street," wrote Lewis Jacobs, "educated in finance, became the overseers of the motion picture business. Characteristic of the new managerial figures were two directors of a new and powerful company, Loew's: W. C. Durant, at that time also head of

General Motors Corporation, and Harvey Gibson, president of the Liberty National Bank.

Wall Street stimulated expansion in other directions besides production at home. For the first time America began its invasion of Europe and other foreign industries, while foreign talent was imported into Hollywood with the double purpose of enriching American movie experience, and impoverishing European industries.

Under the influence of Wall Street too, which (in its interest to protect its investments) preferred real estate to the less tangible collateral of talent and imagination, and saw the importance of organising exhibition on business-like lines, there began a vicious war to gain control of exhibition outlets, to build up great theatre empires. First National on the one hand and Zukor's Famous Players-Lasky on the other, through representatives who often used means comparable only to the techniques of Chicago gangsters, forced small theatre owners throughout the sub-continent to sell out their properties so as to create massive cinema chains.

The invasion of Hollywood by Wall Street had other results. It was no bad thing that efficiency men stepped into regulate some at least of the film industry's extravagance and waste and petty graft. But there were other casualties besides the corrupt and fraudulent and unproductive. Accountants mistrust the unconforming too. Sam Goldwyn, among others, suffered. Guilty of such caprices as importing *Caligari*, he was pushed out of the Presidency of the Goldwyn Company.

Big business left permanent marks on the creative aspects of production. The bureaucrats and accountants, eager to overcome the unpredictable and intractable elements in the creation of films, began to codify certain principles of commercial production that still prevail in the industry: the attempt to exploit proven success with formula pictures and cycles of any particular genre which temporarily sells, at the expense of other and perhaps unorthodox product; the quest for predictable sales values — star names, best-selling success titles, costly and showy production values — which in fact have little to do with art. The supervisor-producer, appointed to oversee production and guard investment by making certain that films conformed to box-office requirements, achieved paramount importance. The Twenties saw, as well as much else, the development of the standardised, assembly-line film and the creation of the myth of "giving the public what it wants." What is astonishing is that so much of real worth came out of this cinema and this era.

★ ★ ★

Practically since the first flicker of a moving picture, the cinema had been a target for moralists. The whole world was thrilled by imagining Hollywood as the Twentieth Century Babylon. On the whole people who made films were working at a demanding craft and were as industrious and ordinary as most other Americans. But as Anita Loos pointed out, "By this time the stars were moving out of the Hollywood Hotel and beginning to live in their own private homes with servants, most of whom were their peers in everything but sex appeal — which pinpoints the reason for the film capital's mass misbehaviour. To place in the limelight a great number of people who ordinarily would be chambermaids and chauffeurs, give them unlimited power and instant wealth, is bound to produce a lively and diverting result." Miss Loos, it must be emphasised, is neither the most reliable nor the most generous observer of the Hollywood scene.

At the very time when movements of increasing strength were pressing for censorship and before notoriety became the true stuff of film publicity, Hollywood suffered from the backlash of several notable scandals. In 1921, in the course of a day-and-night drinking party in a San Francisco hotel a girl called Virginia Rappe became critically ill, and a day or so later died. Roscoe (Fatty) Arbuckle was arrested and charged with manslaughter. The more prurient part of the public gleefully suspected him of the most bestial activities their minds could conjure as taking place between a fat man and a beautiful young girl. After months of trial and retrial the prosecution case collapsed, and Arbuckle was cleared. The public, cheated of their dirt, and the frightened film industry decided none the less to condemn him. His films were withdrawn, and he was never allowed to act again though thanks to one or two loyal and close friends, who included Buster Keaton and Marion Davies, he directed a few films under the name of William Goodrich. While Arbuckle was still on trial, an English-born director of somewhat dubious background was murdered. Mary Miles Minter was discovered to have been in love with the older man (who does not seem to have returned her passion with any intensity) and Mabel Normand was the last person to see him alive. Both girls, though clearly innocent of any connection with the murder, were so smeared by the witch-hunters that one career was ended, the other permanently affected. Mabel Normand was not helped by involvement in a later shooting incident involving her chauffeur. In January 1923 Wallace Reid, the epitome of the handsome, clean-living, all-American hero died as a result of narcotic addiction; and other prominent stars — including the unfortunate Mabel Normand — were rumoured to be fellow users.

These were only the more notorious scandals of the time. All sorts of minor graft and fraud and speculation were exposed. Movie stock — financial as well as moral — fell. The industry sought to save itself by offering a hundred thousand dollars a year to President Harding's Postmaster General, Will Hays, to head a new organisation called the Motion Picture Producers and Distributors of America Inc. for regulation of both the business and the morals of the film industry. Hays zealously applied himself to the task of internal censorship to forestall all the outside bodies who were waiting only too eagerly to tackle the job themselves. It was to take more than four decades before the American cinema escaped from the kindergarten standards of propriety with which the Hays Office hamstrung any attempt to introduce adult themes and adult discussion into pictures.

When Hays took over his job, the industry had hit another period of economic depression. It followed a general, and temporary slump in American business; but it stimulated the consolidation of the industry by a series of mergers in the middle Twenties. Marcus Loew united Goldwyn with Metro, together with Hearst's Cosmopolitan Pictures

rgiastic destruction
' consumer goods:
he Keystone Kops.

Above, Adolph Zukor as The Young Fur Trader at the age of 23.

Right, William Fox as a Golfing American Gentleman.

The director Fred Niblo with (centre) Marcus Loew and (right) Louis B. Mayer.

An "atmospheric" picture palace of the mid-Twenties.

which brought with them the strength of the Hearst Press. Mayer's name was joined in the title of the new organisation.

Zukor and Famous Players-Lasky were investigated by the Federal Trade Commission, but the Commission's two agents who were scheduled to appear with evidence about Zukor's monopolistic activities both claimed to be unable to testify, on health grounds, as the time set for the hearing approached. Will Hays was always credited with the classy public relations work that smoothed over this embarrassment to one of his organisation's members. After the investigation, however, under a plan devised by John Hertz (of Hertz Cars) the Famous Players Theatres were combined with the Balaban and Katz circuits as Publix Theatres, thus nominally divorcing Paramount's production and distribution activities. Other circuits were merged into the great Stanley Company of America. Fox and Universal retained limited exhibition outlets; but the day of the independent theatre owner was past.

★ ★ ★

The war years had seen heightened competition to build grander and grander theatres; and, as evidence of the new refinements, in 1914 the first Wurlitzer organ to boom out for the delight of movie patrons was installed in a cinema in Patterson, New Jersey. The Mark Strand Theatre in New York was the most luxurious and elegant movie house in America, until 1927 when Rothapfel's Roxy, the biggest cinema in the world, with its "Gothic form, renaissance detail and Moorish atmosphere" set new standards. But it was hard to choose between the splendour and extravagance of the theatres that shot up at various times in the Twenties — the Capitol, Loew's State, the Paramount, Radio City Music Hall, the Grauman theatres — with their atmospheric decorations which might, according to the mood of the season or the taste of the architect be in the Moorish or the Egyptian or the Renaissance or the Chinese or the Empire style. Prices had risen accordingly. You might pay 3 or 5 dollars a seat for a Griffith première in the early Twenties; the nickelodeon was a thing of the past.

The social and economic standing of the audience too had changed with the years. Prestige successes like *The Birth of a Nation* and Griffith's subsequent films; the "intellectual" importations from the continent, and the rapid adoption of Chaplin by an intelligentsia who would not have gone near a nickelodeon before the war had drawn in new audiences. The movies were no longer exclusively a cheap entertainment for the poor working masses and non-American-speaking immigrants who were grateful for a purely visual entertainment. Now the cinema was all America's favourite amusement. Besides, this was America's age of plenty: even the working classes and the immigrants had more money to be exploited, higher aspirations to be catered to.

Not that the average mental age of the audience and the average intellectual pretensions of the average filmgoer had risen much. The industry continued to aim at a twelve-year-old level of intelligence. Those like Griffith who tried to aim higher did so at their peril. The majority of the audience were the plain folk of Gopher Prairie, who liked "a good movie, with auto accidents and hold-ups, and some git to it, and not all this talky-talk." When the intellectuals did go to the cinema it was still often in the spirit of larkish, snobby detachment. Amory Blaine (in *This Side of Paradise*) admired his smart college friends who sang and shouted and sent up the films; "Amory decided that he liked the movies, wanted to enjoy them as the row of upper classmen in front had enjoyed them, with their arms along the backs of the seats, their comments Gallic and caustic, their attitude a mixture of critical wit and tolerant amusement."

Film content, none the less, had altered since pre-war days, with changing tastes and the changing social context. Before 1914 the appeal of the cinema to the lower classes was clearly reflected. Settings were characteristically working class; sentiments were characteristically Victorian, with suffering heroines providing for orphan brothers and sisters; sick or dying grandparents, handsome heroes, miraculous benefactors, villains, perils and plot situations inherited from nineteenth-century popular melodrama.

The new middle class audience, the new prosperous working classes, and the will of the conservative business element of America which the film industry so faithfully represented, together conspired to change the characteristic social setting for contemporary film subjects. The films now showed predominantly a wholly imaginary leisured class, with lovely homes and lovely clothes and lovely cars and lovely lives. This was the desired, distorted mirror image of American "normalcy".

The Red Scare provoked a run of films in 1919, one of the most celebrated being Mayflower Films' adaptation of a novel by the notoriously reactionary Thomas Dixon (author of *The Clansman*, on which Griffith had based *The Birth of a Nation*): *Bolshevism on Trial.* Among the rest Universal produced Allen Holubar's *The Right to Happiness*, a Red-*and*-dead tirade; and Joseph M. Schenck presented Chester Withey's *The New Moon* as a vehicle for his wife Norma Talmadge. Closely related were films which depicted malcontent labour being brought to its senses and abandoning strikes in the face of paternalistic capital. On these lines Zukor presented an adaptation of Eugene Walter's play *Paid in Full.* But the rising prosperity of the 1920s clearly provided a more effective bulwark against Bolshevism than either Palmer Raids or film propaganda.

In the post-war circumstances of Hollywood — solidly behind the Republican establishment — it was unlikely that the literary non-conformists, Norris, Dreiser, Mencken, Dos Passos, Sinclair Lewis and so on, would find a very strong echo in the films. Indeed it is surprising that any dissentient voices found a hearing; but they did. Stroheim's *Greed*, of course, was a unique phenomenon; but Vidor's *The Crowd* and Paul Fejos's *Lonesome* introduced refreshing blasts of cool realism into the hothouse of the screen world. At a different level, Cruze's fantasy comedies; at a different level again, Sjöström's tragic *The Wind*; and at a different level again the slapstick assault of the Sennett comedies to a degree undermined the pretences and pretensions of Hollywood's distorting mirror. Warners, too, made *Main Street* (1923) and *Babbitt* (1924) and Famous Players made *Mantrap* (1926), also after Lewis. Even if they were emasculated, the spirit was there.

It would be incorrect to suppose that the new materialism and cynicism of the post-war era entirely swept away the kind of film that depicted and glorified the old heroic and sentimental values. Paradoxically the materialistic society, conforming to the needs and wishes of big business, perpetuated the conservative values of big business alongside the new, liberated ethical and social standards, so that there remained a place for old-fashioned sentimentality like *Way Down East* and *Broken Blossoms*, for Marie Corelli and Hall Caine. Alexandre Bisson's *Madame X* was considered a fairly hoary melodrama when Jane Hading first played it in 1909; it nevertheless survived to be revived twice in the Twenties, with Pauline Frederick in 1920 and with Ruth Chatterton in 1929. Elinor Glyn, the Edwardian English novelist owed her enormous success in Hollywood throughout most of the Twenties to her success in marrying the old romanticism and the new morality in her novels and screenplays. One interesting characteristic of sentimental dramas and sentimental comedies during the earlier part of the period at least is the strange position accorded to women, which seems to be in equal part due to the effect of female emancipation and of defensive male reaction to it. The films have a feminist tendency which is not at all the same as the maternalism that later came to seem so characteristic of American society, though it may be a stage in the progress towards it — an attitude towards the male-female relationship that seems to have derived in equal parts from post-war emancipation and from post-war fictional images of the wife and mother as the one whose lot is to suffer and to atone.

Throughout practically every film of the class it is the woman who is adoring, devoted, faithful, sacrificing; the man who philanders and allows himself to be distracted and seduced by the The Wrong Girl. In *Stage Struck*, for instance, Gloria Swanson as the little waitress does Lawrence Gray's laundry and even buys him new shirts, while he flirts with show-boat actresses. In *Love 'Em and Leave 'Em* the same actor is a window display man who secures promotion on the strength of ideas given him by the self-effacing Evelyn Brent. In the nature of things Hollywood love, of course, always triumphs in the end.

Most characteristic are the films which express — with self-conscious enthusiasm and narcissism which are still attractive in themselves — the new social and moral standards of the post-war era, The Roaring Twenties, the Jazz Age. Social comedies and domestic dramas found their motives in the new, post-Freud fascination with sex, the emancipation of American women, the working girl, the discarding of old codes of manners as of ethics, the slackening of marital ties. They found their characteristic images in short skirts, short hair, country clubs, night clubs, speakeasies, cocktail parties, the extravagances of Jazz-Modern interior decoration. The cycle was begun, of course, by DeMille as early as 1919; and he was followed by every other American director and literally hundreds of films with titillating titles and ultra-modern content. With the arrival of Lubitsch in America in 1922 a new delicacy and sophistication and detachment and continental wickedness was contributed to the form. Earlier von Stroheim's *Blind Husbands* and *Foolish Wives* injected a note of brutality and realism into films about marital relationships.

The fascination of these films today is to see the age's own image of itself, to see how the films dramatised and fostered the aspirations of the business age; urged consumption as a way of life in a society which depended upon consumption by showing a social setting in which cars and clothes and elaborate decors, expensive elegance and a get-rich-quick life of luxury and hectic leisure were a desirable norm.

It was characteristic of Hollywood's double thinking as of the dilemma of the times that these Jazz Age films almost invariably find the *dénouement* of their modern plot problems in the old morality. The Dancing Daughters and flappers and It Girls all end up married and adjusted to a respectable middle class future: the erring wives come back to patient husbands. There are refreshing exceptions. In *Dancing Mothers*, for instance, Alice Joyce leaves her Dancing Husband and Dancing Daughter for ever and a new life, away from the Dancing World.

The underworld that belonged so inextricably to the Jazz Age was inevitably reflected on the screen. DeMille characteristically was responsible, as producer, for an early example of the *genre*, Frank Urson's *Chicago*, adapted by Lenore Coffee from a stage play by

Maurice Watkins. The most distinguished early gangster films were unquestionably the von Sternberg series (*Underworld*, *The Drag Net*, *The Docks of New York*) and Lewis Milestone's *The Racket*. Gangster films were however to reach their notable peak in the next decade.

At the start of the post-war decade, war films were distinctly out of favour, though two delayed films which arrived so near the Armistice as to be practically post-war releases enjoyed success — *Hearts of the World* on Griffith's prestige; *Shoulder Arms* as a great film of irresistible appeal and — in the way Chaplin metamorphosed the realities of war into comic fantasy — considerably more meaningful than the majority of war films that had preceded it. *The Four Horsemen of the Apocalypse* (1921) got by more on extraneous sources of glamour and on the current fashion for Ibañez novels than as a war subject. The picture it represented in any case reflected the popular home sentiments of vengeance by depicting the conflict in cruelly hard blacks and whites. Four years later, in 1925, Vidor's *The Big Parade* revealed that there was once again a box-office for war films; and its success, together with changed attitudes after the Locarno Pact, accounted for a flurry of war films in 1926-7.

America's favourite source of action on the screen was the Western. The West represented urban America's dream of lost innocence, of a pastoral freedom now sacrificed to hustle and the motor car. There was a parallel tendency to explode the myth: films like Fairbanks's *Manhattan Madness*, *Wild and Woolly* and *The Mollycoddle* contrasted the Easterner's dream of the West with the reality — a West that had largely vanished even by this time. In *Wild and Woolly*, the hero, a West-mad office-bound youth visits an Easternised Western town whose inhabitants get together to re-create "the Old West" for his benefit. Even here the film-makers could not quite bring themselves to kill the myth and the hero finds himself in the middle of *real* Wild West adventures, just like the hero of *The Mollycoddle* (1920), a young man brought up in the decadent atmosphere of Europe who nevertheless finds his Western ruggedness aroused when he returns to the home of his ancestors.

The debunking was not, in fact, either basic or permanent; and by the early Twenties the Western had passed into its classic period, when the perennial formulas of the genre were laid down. Like almost any great tradition in popular drama, the Western has only one plot. Its appeal lies in the reassuringly recognisable form and force and morality of the story; its art consists in the skill with which variations are developed upon basic themes.

The essential *scenario* (in the *commedia dell'arte* sense rather than the film meaning of the word) offers us a good man, who opposes a bad man who is corrupting or terrorising the locality. The bad man is generally also the good man's rival for the girl whom the good man loves, the bad man lusts for. And the bad man is likely to be abetted by the girl's uncle or guardian. The story is spun about these facts, about the bad man's foils to destroy or discredit the good man; the perils which are put in the way of the girl; the eventual defeat of the bad man through the moral and physical superiority of the hero.

The historical setting can be the period of colonisation (*Winners of the Wilderness*, 1927), the Indian Wars (*The Red Raiders*, 1927), the land rush (*Tumbleweeds*, 1925; *The Covered Wagon*, 1923), the opening up of the continent (*The Pony Express*, 1925), the building of the great trans-continental railways (*The Iron Horse*, 1924), the gold rushes, the suppression of banditry, the cleaning up of civic corruption in the mushrooming communities. Within it the plot and basic characters are as unvariable as the Victorian pantomime.

There were other outlets too for the frustrated romanticism of the Jazz Age. The studios had for years put an embargo on costume films when Fairbanks suddenly enjoyed immense success with the series of films that began with *The Mark of Zorro*, and Valentino forced a new image on the Twenties with *The Sheik*. There was a seemingly unstemmable flow of desert romances and every historical period and exotic locale was explored to provide vehicles for new romantic heroes and heroines like Novarro and Moreno and Mary Astor and Vilma Banky. There were stories of Renaissance Italy, of Revolutionary France, of Elizabethan England, of Catherine's Russia. The durability of this sort of escapism — escapism now from the moral and psychological complexities of modern life as pre-war escapism had been from the economic struggles of the American worker — is evidenced by the fact that Warner Brothers' choice of subject for their first all-synchronised film was *Don Juan*, starring John Barrymore and Mary Astor.

The spectacle film, which had gone somewhat out of fashion after the commercial failure of *Intolerance* and the economic pressures of the immediate post-war period, enjoyed a considerable revival in the mid-Twenties, with the DeMille mammoths *The Ten Commandments* and *King of Kings*, but more particularly after the monumental *Ben Hur*, in 1926. (The film had been begun by Metro years before, in Italy, with the intention of re-establishing the pre-war prosperity of the Italian studios. When they found that shooting in Italy was more costly even than in Hollywood, the Americans retreated rapidly, scrapping sets director, stars and material already shot. The final cost to M-G-M was estimated at over six million dollars.)

Perhaps the popularity of the anthropological or pseudo-anthropological documentary in the Twenties was a sign of another direction of escapism — the appeal of primitive societies free from the neurotic stresses of modern civilisation. The comparative success of Flaherty's *Nanook* took its distributors by surprise and encouraged William Fox to commission *Moana*; while Merian C. Cooper and Ernest Schoedsack's *Grass* popularised the travel film generally.

Newsreels had become important in the War; and in the Twenties each of the major movie empires had its own news: Zukor had Paramount; Universal, International and Loews, Hearst Metrotone News. They were of especial importance for cementing the cinema's political connections. Mayer bound Hoover's affections to himself by the crucial support the Hearst newsreels had given to Hoover's election campaign; and the President's friendship was to prove lasting and valuable to M-G-M.

A minor but popular feature of Hollywood production was the animated cartoon, already, since before the war, a regular element in supporting programmes. Mutt and Jeff, originated in 1917, continued throughout the silent period. Pat Sullivan's Felix the Cat, animated by Otto Mesmer, was as characteristic a personality of the Twenties as Valentino or Aimée MacPherson. Max Fleischer created Koko the Clown, who was inclined to co-star with human actors in his films; and Walt Disney was at work from 1925, producing the *Alice in Cartoonland* series, the *Oswald the Lucky Rabbit* series, and, on the eve of sound, Mortimer (later Mickey) Mouse.

★ ★ ★

By 1918 the art of film-making had become more sophisticated and complex than a pre-war producer could have imagined; and by the end of the post-war decade — though especially with the advent of sound — the craft had become still more skilled and subtle. Up till the war, practically any actor could step behind the camera and take over the direction of a film — which, indeed, is how the great majority of directors recruited before the war started in their craft. Now the director's job was increasingly demanding, as film technique was sophisticated, first by the staggering developments in method pioneered by Griffith, and by the increasing use of the mobile camera (before the war the bulk of films were still essentially photographed charades); later by the examples of the continental film-makers, but notably the Germans and Soviets. Aside from the purely technical resourcefulness now demanded of a director, Thomas Ince's view of the desiderata of the good director remain valid: "The ideal director is one who, having pictured a scene in his mind, having tested it by putting himself into the various roles and getting reactions to those characters, still allows his cast enough scope to bring out additional touches that will add spontaneity to the interpretation and dramatic up-building. . . . Primarily the director must know life, but he must know, too, how to project life, not in narrative form, but by selected dramatic moments, each of which builds towards a definite crisis or climax that will bring a burst of emotional response from every audience."

Ince himself — though his historical significance is somewhat clouded by a vanity that made him claim the achievements of others as his own — seems to have been the ideal creative producer. But the marriage of Hollywood and Wall Street, as has already been suggested, saw the rise of the supervisor-producer whose interest was rather accountancy than artistic considerations.

A more positive development was the increasing importance of the writer. Before the war a good deal of shooting was done "off the cuff". Griffith never used a script, and it is Ince who is generally credited with the innovation of the written scenario as a standard preliminary to shooting. Larger budgets, longer and more costly film projects demanded a higher degree of pre-planning; and the scenarist began to achieve an importance almost as great as that of the director. A surprising number of the most successful scenarists of silent days were women — Metro's June Mathis, who devised the best Valentino vehicles and died only a year after the star; Frances Marion, Mary Pickford's favourite writer who later scripted such distinguished films as *The Scarlet Letter* and *The Wind*; Anita Loos, the child prodigy who at fifteen was supplying the Biograph Studios with ingenious story ideas; DeMille's Jeanie Macpherson; Bess Meredith and Lenore Coffee, better known as a writer of talking pictures. Among the innumerable male scenarists were Jules Furthman who wrote Sternberg's *Underworld* and Stiller's *Hotel Imperial*, Howard Estabrook and Benjamin Glazer.

Soon after the war producers began their long-maintained policy of trying to achieve prestige for their productions by attracting authors of distinction to work in Hollywood. In 1920 Lasky invited Maeterlinck, Edward Knoblock and Somerset Maugham among others. Few stayed long, once they discovered that "All authors, living or dead, famous or obscure, shared the same fate. Their stories were re-written and completely altered either by the stenographers and continuity girls of the scenario department, or by the Assistant Director and his lady-love, or by the leading lady, or by anyone else who happened to pass through the studio; and even when at last after infinite struggle a scene was shot which bore some resemblance to the original story it was certain to be left out in the cutting-room, or pared away to such an extent that all meaning which it might once have had was lost."

Elinor Glyn, who wrote this, was one of those who stayed on. Unpredictably, the sensational Edwardian English novelist, nearly sixty when she arrived in Hollywood, stayed there for years, made (and partly spent) a fortune, achieved new fame and, sending the gospel of "It" across the world, had immense influence upon the film capital. For one thing she claimed to have taught American screen heroes how to make love. Valentino learned from Glyn to kiss the *palm* of a woman's hand. Her insistence upon accurate staging of the worlds she portrayed awoke designers to new responsibilities.

It is worth parenthetically tracing Glyn's Hollywood career, for several of her successes exerted considerable influence on favourite film themes of the Twenties. She worked industriously, turning novels into films and film scenarios into novels which — thanks to her exposure to the cinema — acquired a dash her earlier work had lacked. *The Great Moment* (1921), directed by Sam Wood, starred Gloria Swanson as the daughter of an English aristocrat whose gipsy blood tended to come out rather embarrassingly in moments of stress. *Beyond the Rocks* (1922), again directed by Sam Wood, had Swanson falling in love with an English lord played by Valentino. After this Glyn left Lasky for Goldwyn to make a somewhat expurgated version of *Three Weeks* (1924), directed by Alan Crosland and starring Aileen Pringle and Conrad Nagel. (This was not the first version of the novel. One Perry N. Vekroff had adapted it earlier for the Reliable Feature Film Corporation in 1915.) At Metro-Goldwyn King Vidor filmed *His Hour* (1924), apparently competently and despite Mrs. Glyn's supervision. *Six Days* (1923), directed by Charles Brabin, has a plot silly enough to recall. Among other complications the hero and heroine visit the French battlefields where they are trapped in a dug-out after the girl steps on an unexploded bomb. Fortunately they have with them an old *curé* who marries them before dying of his wounds; and for six days they are left to make love and dig their way out by turns. On being rescued, the hero for some reason makes off while the girl is swooning; but returns in a hectic race by 'plane, car and bareback horse in the nick of time to save her from marrying the wrong man.

After three more films of almost comparable extravagance (*Man and Maid*, *Love's Blindness* and *The Only Thing*), Miss Glyn returned to Famous Players-Lasky, now Paramount. Her first script, *Ritzy*, is said to have been unusually silly, the story of an American girl in Paris. But it was followed by her two American triumphs, influenced by her discovery of the enchanting Clara Bow — *It* and *Red Hair*, both directed with considerable wit by Clarence Badger, the second, suitably, in colour.

The title writer too came into greater prominence. The child Anita Loos appears to have been one of the first people to demonstrate how much intelligent titling can contribute to a film. Sometimes the sub-titles, as they were called, have weathered less well than the pictures they accompany. Literary pretensions and topical jokes can date them embarrassingly. But, at their best (in *It* for instance, and most of Keaton's films) the titles authentically catch the idiom of the times, or one is struck by the skill with which the typography and layout carries the emphasis and stresses which an actor in a talking film would be able to convey by speech. Like the film cutter, who in this period began to take more and more of the responsibility of editing from the director (though artists like Keaton, Chaplin, Laurel and Vidor continued to cut their own films), the titles could do a good deal towards patching up an inadequate film.

Silent film photography was lucky in inheriting the high craft traditions of late Victorian art photography. Refinements in stock, equipment and lighting, and the influence of the German expressionist cinema combined to make Hollywood cameramen in the Twenties the most expert in the world. Maurice Tourneur, Rex Ingram and von Sternberg were among the most important directors who made special demands upon their cameramen. The distinguished cameramen of these years are almost innumerable. Among the greatest, photographers whose style is as identifiable and memorable as that of a painter, were Charles Rosher (*Sunrise*, *Tempest*), William Daniels, Garbo's most sympathetic cameraman, Bert Glennon, who shot *Hotel Imperial* and many Sternberg features, George Barnes, who worked with Henry King, John Arnold (*The Wind*), Gilbert Warrenton, known particularly for his brilliant handling of the mobile camera, Arthur Edeson, Jackson Rose, Joe August, Lucien Andriot, Tony Gaudio, Lee Garmes (another Sternberg collaborator), Oliver Marsh (brother of Mae Marsh and especially renowned for his ability to recapture the bloom of fading stars), George Schneidermann, who majestically photographed a number of Ford pictures, including *The Iron Horse*.

New credits began to appear on film titles as a result of the growing complexity of production techniques. The doyen of art directors is Cedric Gibbons who began his work in films with Edison in 1914, joining Goldwyn in 1918 after military service, and passing to M-G-M, where he stayed, to become supervising art director, in 1924. Generally the creative art director began to make his appearance around 1919. Paramount was reckoned to have the strongest art department in the early years of the period, and captured a considerable prize when the German designer Hans Dreier was brought over in 1923. Van Nest Polglase, an art director from 1919, joined Paramount in 1927. Albert D'Agostino worked successively for Metro, Selznick and his own Tec-Art Studios; in the following decade he was to work for Universal and R.K.O. Make-up, too, became important as films passed into an era of greater technical refinement and dramatic subtlety. The greatest influence in the Twenties in this department of studio work was the already veteran make-up artist Max Factor, with his theory of "colour harmony" in cosmetics.

At its best — in the work of Lillian Gish or Garbo or Barthelmess or Keaton or in unpredictable flashes of brilliance in Valentino — screen acting for silent films had developed into an art, new and unique, which was lost when pictures spoke. Actors were obliged to develop new means of expression. Ince wrote, "Do any but those who are intimately familiar with the stage world and its art realise the tremendous loss of power the actor of the silent drama suffers because his voice is stilled? After all, is there any ability more remarkable than that of the gifted actor who, without the aid of the emotion-rousing voice and the power of flesh and blood presence, can so project a characterisation that the figments of some author's brain come to life for audiences gathered from every walk of life and numbering millions? Thought becomes reality — that is the world's greatest marvel.

"To act a part an actor must feel it deeply, and so carry this feeling in his consciousness that, when he plays the scene, his reactions are instinctive. The pantomime of eyes, mouth, hands and bodily movement will seem unconscious if the actor is thinking and feeling the part. . . . It is only when the screen actor has become a past master of the art of pantomime that the audience is lulled into the oblivion of illusion."

The silent actors were serious about their work. Lillian Gish starved for days before she shot the final scene of *La Bohème*. Mary Pickford studied to achieve the deportment of a girl who had spent her youth carrying smaller children about. Their methods of innervation, of working themselves into the mood and feeling of a role had all the intensity and sincerity of the Stanislavski studios. Mack Sennett recalled that Mabel Normand "insisted on working on a stage to the accompaniment of the loudest jazz syncopation the record library could provide. Other actresses, particularly such dramatic stars as Mae Marsh, Mary Garden, the opera star, Madge Kennedy, Marie Doro, Maxine Elliott and Jane Cowl, were put in the proper mood by the sobbing of soft violins. Not Mabel. She wanted action."

The art of the silent screen actor deserves a study of its own; but even that could never wholly explain the magic of Garbo's scene with the bouquet in *A Woman of Affairs* or Gish's frenzy in *The Wind.*

3. Survivors

THE WAR marked the most complete transition in the history of the cinema, apart from the introduction of sound; and it is significant that although practically all the artists who came to maturity in the course of the Twenties were recruited to the cinema in the years either side of 1914, few of those who were *prominently* active before that date had any great success after the war. Edwin Porter retired from film-making in 1915 and devoted himself to marketing cameras until he was ruined in the crash of 1929. Colin Campbell, the Scottish *émigré* director, continued to make films until 1924, but never recaptured the success of *The Spoilers* (1914) or *The Crisis* (1916). George Baker, director of the John Bunny comedies, became a supervisor at Metro and disappeared from view.

Among those who did weather the transition, as later, after the 1929 crash, he was able to weather the larger revolution and find work (albeit modest) once again in the industry, was **JAMES STUART BLACKTON.** English-born, Blackton was a pioneer of 1896, when he made some of the first animated drawings for Vitascope. He was a notable innovator in the primitive years; and later, during the war, made a number of good propaganda films, including *Womanhood* (1917), *The Common Cause* (1917) and *Safe for Democracy* (1917). After the war Blackton spent a brief period in England, where he revealed a taste for costume pageants: *A Gypsy Cavalier* (1922), *The Glorious Adventure* (1922), *The Virgin Queen* (1923). (The last two films were experiments in colour and their dull, static quality may be due to over-concern with technical problems.) Back in Hollywood Blackton continued to work for his own old firm, Vitagraph, until it was absorbed by Warners. A practised craftsman with an ability to adjust to prevailing fashion, Blackton, who was in any case always somewhat distracted by business interests, was never really appreciated as a creative artist. Among his post-war films *Beloved Brutes* and *Tides of Passion* are said to be extremely good.

The post-war career of **SIDNEY OLCOTT** was considerably more lively. Olcott had arrived on the scene later than Blackton, recruited as an actor by Mutoscope in 1904. He became General Manager at Biograph, and then Kalem's first director. He made history with his *Ben Hur* (1907) which attracted the first copyright action against the movies, and lost the Kalem Company a good deal of money in damages. A pioneer director of Westerns, Canadian-born Olcott was also the first American director to make a point of working abroad whenever the opportunity presented itself. He shot the first story-films to be made in Ireland, and worked in most countries of Europe. In 1912 he shot *From the Manger to the Cross* in Palestine.

His activity continued through the war years and became no less eclectic. After the war he showed himself still a highly responsible craftsman and an assured commercial director. In these later years he showed a special facility for adapting stage successes to the screen as star vehicles. Thus his *Little Old New York*, made for William Randolph Hearst's company, established Marion Davies as an authentic star comedienne. He directed George Arliss in William Archer's *The Green Goddess* (1923), Valentino in Booth Tarkington's *Monsieur Beaucaire* (1924), Swanson in *The Humming Bird* (1924), and Pola Negri in *The Charmer* (1925). The following year he directed Richard Barthelmess in three of the most successful films the star made outside his work for Griffith and King: *Ranson's Folly*, *The White Black Sheep*, *The Amateur Gentleman*. In 1927 Olcott came to London to work for British Lion, against whom he was awarded judgement in a curious action brought because he refused to make films tending "to glorify crime". After this, at the age of 54, he definitively retired, one of the most energetic, active and resourceful figures of the cinema's early years.

The most distinguished survivor was, of course, **D. W. GRIFFITH**, whose reputation at the end of the war was at its zenith. Griffith was the cinema's first international celebrity, for a time attracting a more universal respect even than his co-founders of United Artists, Chaplin, Pickford and Fairbanks. The total transformation of the American

The four United Artists: Fairbanks, Griffith, Mary Pickford and Chaplin, circa 1919.

D. W. Griffith directing INTOLERANCE. Bitzer and the camera; Bessie Love in background.

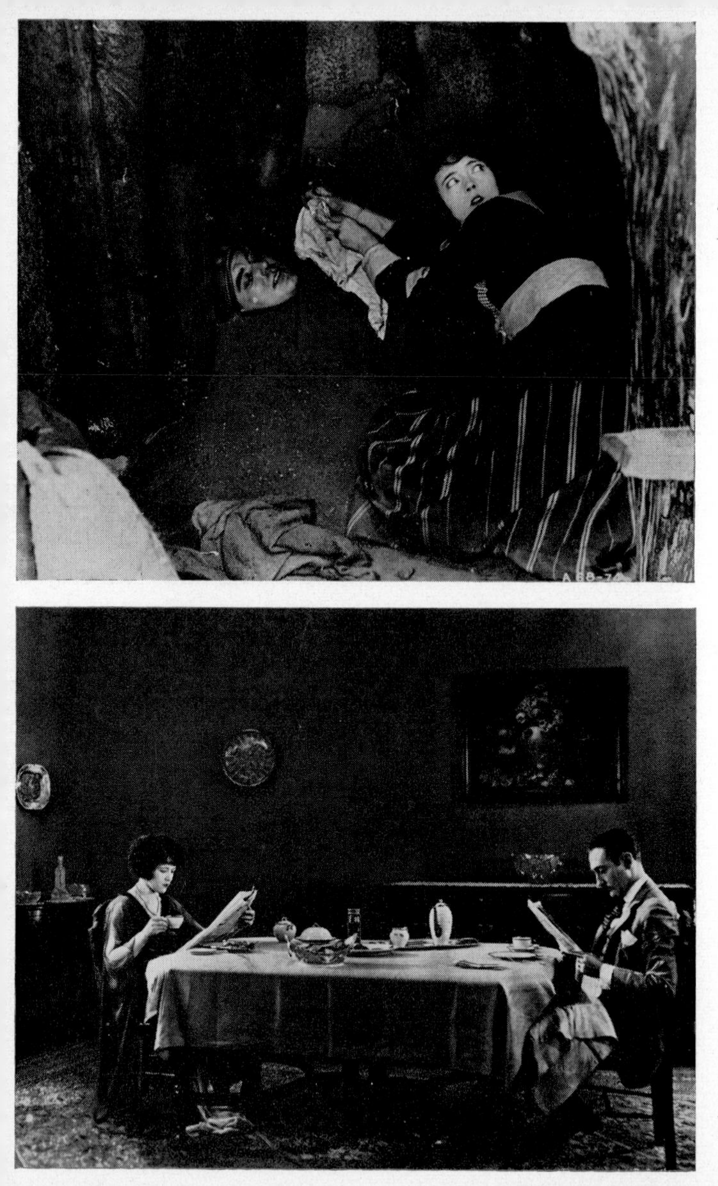

Lillian Gish in D. W. Griffith's THE GREATEST THING IN LIFE (1918), seemingly undertaken as a government propaganda film.

Marie Prevost and Adolphe Menjou in Ernst Lubitsch's THE MARRIAGE CIRCLE (1924), a satirical comedy of manners told by pictorial means with a minimum of sub-titles.

film from primitivism to art in the decade before 1918 was largely due to Griffith alone.

The history of this strange and remarkable man is well enough known: the aristocratic Southern background; the celebrity of his father, "Roaring" Jake Griffith, a hero of the Civil War; the post-Civil War impoverishment of the family; the years as a struggling actor and aspiring author; the alternation of successes like the sale of the play *A Fool and a Girl* (1907) and the more frequent failures; the final humiliation of the unemployed actor seeking work in the despised moving pictures; the film début in *Rescued From an Eagle's Nest*, directed by Edwin Porter, whose mantle as an innovator of film narrative techniques was to descend to Griffith.

He began to sell stories to Biograph, and in 1908 directed his first one-reeler, *The Adventures of Dollie*. His stories were intelligent and lucid; and their immediate appeal to the public helped restore Biograph's fading fortunes. Griffith kept busy for several years turning out two films a week, most often with the collaboration of his loyal and clever cameraman Billy Bitzer. What is remarkable is that through this prolific period Griffith, instead of growing stale in his techniques, continued to experiment and learn and augment his technical and artistic means. Between 1908 and 1914 Griffith gave the cinema its syntax practically complete. He developed Porter's innovation of cross-cutting. He introduced cutting within the scene as a standard practice. He introduced realistic and expressive lighting. He used masks and irises to make the very shape of the screen an instrument for dramatic expression. He increased the range of the camera's vision — used close-ups, which enabled actors to work more subtly and detail to be more immediately revealing, and long-shots which emancipated the film from the stall's-eye view of earlier cinema drama. He released the screen image from a simply two-dimensional movement and gave it perspective, foreground and background. He used the moving camera (actually a familiar, if disorganised device from the earliest days) for dramatic purposes. From the theatre he brought concepts of pace and timing. He also recruited a new kind of actor — fresh youngsters whose smooth faces could stand up to close-ups, and whose acting styles were still innocent of the heavy and mannered habits of the Victorian stage. Among the talents first introduced into the studios by Griffith were Pickford, the Gish sisters, Bessie Love, Blanche Sweet, Richard Barthelmess, Robert Harron, Mae Marsh.

Griffith not only enlarged the cinema's language but also its range of subjects. *The Song of the Shirt* and *A Corner in Wheat* attempted social questions, even if at a simple level. He embarked on his first historico-philosophical spectacles, such as *Judith of Bethulia*. To suit more sophisticated subjects he made films in greater length than had hitherto been customary. At four reels, *Judith of Bethulia* was the longest film made until that time.

In five years Griffith had made himself the unchallenged master of the medium that he had made over. In late 1913 he left Biograph for Reliance Majestic, releasing through Mutual. Although Griffith made four preliminary pictures there, his whole attention was concentrated on *The Birth of a Nation* (1915), in which, absolutely deliberately and consciously, he set out to create "the greatest picture ever made". It was so; and it remains the most important and influential in film history, introducing audiences as it did to experiences they had never known before, compelling acceptance of the motion pictures as an unparalleled means of communication, and a genuine form of art.

The immense profits from *The Birth of a Nation* were poured into his next film *Intolerance* (1916), in which Griffith had "conferred both magnitude and complexity as well as expressiveness on the motion pictures" (Iris Barry: "D. W. Griffith: American Film Master", N.Y., Museum of Modern Art). A film of immense formative importance in the history of the cinema, *Intolerance* was never a commercial success; and Griffith spent many years painfully restoring debts the film had incurred. In 1917 he had gone to Europe to make *Hearts of the World*, a film intended originally to help bring America into the war, but which appeared only a few months before the Armistice in 1918. One more film, now entirely lost, *The Great Love*, about the galvanising of pre-war social butterflies into the war effort, completed his war-time activity. In the meantime he had become a successful producer of, among other films, the series of light comedies starring Dorothy Gish.

It is worth recalling Griffith's past career at this length in order to assess his stock at the end of the war. He had enjoyed an international prestige equalled by no one else in the cinema. He had created his own artistic medium — the paramount means of expression of the twentieth century. He had created the cinema's first universally recognised masterpieces. At the same time he was no business man and he was burdened with the debts incurred by *Intolerance* (the Wark Producing Company was to go bankrupt in 1921). He was, at bottom, inseparably wedded to the nineteenth century — its literature, its drama, its tastes and its morals. He was on the verge of being overtaken by the cinema which he had done so much to create, by the post-war world in which at first he stood as a giant. His situation is summed up by Mrs. Eileen Bowser in her supplement to the Museum of Modern Art's monograph: "Brought up in poverty and without adequate education, Griffith had aspirations to be a great writer, in particular a great playwright. Now he was hailed as the Shakespeare of the screen and he walked with the great of his time, the wealthy and the socially prominent. Although he knew that he had poured his heart into *The Birth of a Nation* and *Intolerance*, he must have been a bit bewildered to have achieved such success in the medium he had originally despised. His was an intuitive genius, and fame made him self-conscious. His deliberate striving for artistic excellence or for popularity in his later films led him at times to descend into mannerism. The financial failure of *Intolerance* made him painfully aware of the need to cater more to popular taste, yet he was never sure of what popular taste was."

But for the moment he had confidence, prestige and a great actress, Lillian Gish. *A Romance of Happy Valley*, Griffith's first post-war release, was evidently a relaxation, a return to the simple anecdotes of Biograph days and to the Kentucky of his boyhood memory. No copy of this film or his next, *The Greatest Thing in Life* (1918) exists, unfortunately, today. Lillian Gish has said that it is impossible to evaluate Griffith without knowing this latter film. The climactic scene in which a white boy kisses a dying negro soldier (on the lips, according to Miss Gish, though Mrs. Bowser says on the cheek) appears to have been unfailingly startling to all who saw it, and a striking refutation of ideas of Griffith's racism. (The racist aspect of his work accords uncomfortably with other aspects of Griffith's personality. It undeniably exists in *The Birth of a Nation* and in hints elsewhere in the work. At best it can be written off as being the effect of inherited habits of thought, innocently unquestioned, rather than positive and maliciously maintained opinion.) Both *The Greatest Thing in Life* and *The Girl Who Stayed at Home* (1919) seem to have been undertaken as government propaganda films. Griffith was at this time busy working off a contract with Zukor's Artcraft Company, and his next two films were made quickly, though conscientiously. *True Heart Susie* (1919) was another sentimental retreat to rural America, with a sweet performance by Lillian Gish, but it was hopelessly outmoded in the year that saw the release of DeMille's *Don't Change Your Husband.* A Western, *Scarlet Days* (1919), starring Richard Barthelmess, sounds attractive, but all prints of it have disappeared.

Even now Griffith had masterpieces in him. *Broken Blossoms* (1919), adapted from a short story in Thomas Burke's *Limehouse Nights*, was, incredibly, made in eighteen days (though Griffith's method called for a lot of prior rehearsal — a method which Miss Gish long maintained after she had left Griffith). However much the techniques which Griffith pioneered in this film were abused by later film-makers, his success in producing richly evocative and poetic atmosphere and imagery is undeniable. The soft-focus photography, the eerie studio-manufactured London fogs still work upon the spectator, and are a tribute to Billy Bitzer's endlessly resourceful camerawork for Griffith.* The performances of Gish as the little slum girl, Donald Crisp as her brutal father and Richard Barthelmess as the spiritual Chinese boy who falls in love with her and tries to save her are still as compelling as any surviving silent screen performances.

*Kevin Brownlow points out that the soft-focus effects were actually the trade-mark of Hendrik Sartov, who was brought in on this picture.

Griffith was working at full pressure to re-establish his commercial independence and to build his new studios at Mamaroneck. *Broken Blossoms* was released through United Artists, which had been founded in 1919; but *The Greatest Question* (1919), a drama about spiritualism, and *The Idol Dancer* and *The Love Flower*, both exotic melodramas, were made for First National. For the first time in these films, Griffith seems to have been repeating himself, working with a slackened enthusiasm and inspiration. He recovered his forces completely however for *Way Down East* (1920) which is, perhaps, the masterpiece among the later films, still completely valid despite the anachronism of the subject — perhaps indeed by the very reason of Griffith's fidelity to a period which was already past but which was essentially his own. His purchase of the rights of Lottie Blair Parker's creaky old play at a cost of $175,000 was a matter of incredulity and ridicule at the time; but the film proved more popular than any Griffith work since *The Birth of a Nation.* At risk of the life and limb of every member of the unit (but particularly poor Lillian Gish who had to be defrosted constantly after exposure on the ice floes) Griffith shot the film with startling realism, the exteriors being filmed on the frozen Connecticut River. This, together with the integrity of the performances of Barthelmess and the incomparable Gish (the baptism of the dying child is still one of the most moving episodes in the history of the cinema) explain the lasting success of the film.

Still Griffith was borne on by the tide of success. *Dream Street* (1921), an attempt to repeat the success of *Broken Blossoms* with two more Burke stories, was a failure on all counts, despite some precocious experiments with synchronised sound. But *Orphans of the Storm* (1921) was a critical success and one of the best American costume spectacles of the era — rivalling those of Lubitsch which were at that time being imported from Germany with considerable prestige. The performances of the Gish girls are legendary. Mrs. Bowser relates that many spectators actually thought they heard Dorothy singing, so vivid was Lillian's acting in the scene where, searching for her blind sister, she at last hears her voice, distantly singing in the streets. The cost of the film had, however, been immense. Griffith proceeded with the same extravagance as on *Intolerance*: the sets of revolutionary Paris covered thirteen acres. It was impossible for the film to recoup such a cost. After this, no Griffith film ever made a profit. It seemed as if Griffith's luck turned when Lillian Gish left him, to be replaced by Carol Dempster, a much less accountable actress who nevertheless seemed to exert a fascination over Griffith.

One Exciting Night (1922) did as well commercially as any of the later films, and is memorable as a pioneer murder-mystery drama. It was followed by *The White Rose* (1923), a sentimental piece with little but pretty camerawork and a good performance by Mae Marsh to recommend it.

It would be interesting to see *America* (1924), in which Griffith returned to the theme of American history, which had intrigued him since *The Massacre* (1912). He himself felt that the film suffered because the history was insufficiently leavened with personalised stories. Later critics have felt the contrary, that the sentimental intrigues involving Carol Dempster and Neil Hamilton get in the way of the sweep of spectacle, for which Griffith evidently still kept his talent. *Isn't Life Wonderful* (1924) is considered by those who have seen it to be one of Griffith's most mature works. Made on location in Germany, on the theme of the effects of war's aftermath upon ordinary human beings, it can, says Mrs. Bowser, be compared with Italian neo-realism of the immediate post-World War Two years — and this despite a tacked-on happy ending. She adds, "For Griffith it was to be the last great film, after which he gave up his long fought-for independence and went to work as an employee of Adolph Zukor."

The rest of Griffith's career is a short story. Surprisingly it was his own idea to shoot a film version of the stage success *Poppy* as *Sally of the Sawdust* (1925); and though neither he nor the redoubtable W. C. Fields thought the other particularly funny, the results were much better than might have been expected. Fields, despite the (to him, severe) handicap of silence, successfully carried his performance over from the stage; the play itself was clean-cut and quick-moving; and Griffith seems to have enjoyed the recollection of barn-storming days. No print apparently exists of the second film with Fields, *That Royle Girl* (1926). Griffith's last film for Zukor, *The Sorrows of Satan* (1926) — Marie Corelli's novel had originally been bought for DeMille who had in the meantime parted from Paramount — was a financial disaster though critics who have seen it recently describe the film as brilliant. Paramount bought up the rest of Griffith's contract, and he returned to United Artists, with Nicholas Schenck financing his productions through the Art Cinema Corporation. But Griffith had lost confidence, and perhaps other qualities besides. *Drums of Love* (1928) was a sex picture of no obvious merit. *The Battle of the Sexes* (1928), in which he pathetically tried to remake and recapture his success of fifteen years earlier, seems to have been deplorable from every point of view. *Lady of the Pavements*, with a theme reminiscent of Diderot's *Jacques le fataliste*, a synchronised score and Lupe Velez did rather better. As the silent period closed, Griffith, once the giant of the American cinema, had been reduced to a has-been, an anachronism, unwanted in the new Hollywood.

Sound revived his curiosity and interest in the medium. *Abraham Lincoln* seems to have been inventive and intermittently good; and *The Struggle* (1931), again according to Mrs. Bowser, a good deal better than contemporary opinion would suggest. But it was too late. Griffith withdrew into a retirement that ended only with his death in 1948. He occasionally spoke of comebacks; and to the end of his life he kept tinkering with a dramatic epic which he had begun more than forty years before, and which was never realised.

4. Invaders

THE WAR YEARS had immensely strengthened the commercial situation of the American cinema by practically removing foreign competition. At the same time isolation had confirmed certain pre-war characteristics of American films. The inhabitants of Main Street, Gopher Prairie were conservative and prosaic people who preferred a good yarn to poetry or ideas and were mistrustful of any sort of fancy or artistic pretensions. So while film-makers in France, Germany, and Sweden were discovering new artistic dimensions — the film's potentialities for exploring psychology and atmosphere, for lyricism and for new sensory and visual experiences — the American cinema had settled in its ways of being primarily a story-telling medium. The characteristics of the pre-war cinema still prevailed to a large extent: the predominance of narrative; the dominance of literary and dramatic traditions; an exclusively objective vision of the world on the screen. The American cinema grew out of the nineteenth-century novel and the nineteenth-century theatre — the native theatre of Belasco rather than that of Ibsen and Shaw and Stanislavski. Before the war the principal foreign influences had been the French *films d'art* and the Italian spectacles. Griffith, it is true, had immeasurably enriched the means of cinematic expression; but Griffith was by origin and persuasion a story-teller from the Belasco theatre; and behind all his experiments in form had been a first loyalty to narrative. Griffith was bent on discovering better ways of telling the story; and, of course, he found them.

In the Twenties, however, the horizons of the American film-maker were dramatically enlarged by the importation first of foreign films, and later, in massive bulk, of foreign artists. In the cinema of 1918 native Americans predominated. *Foreigners like Maurice Tourneur

*Kevin Brownlow points out that before the war there was a considerable influx of French film people — Gasnier, Tourneur, Andriot, Guissart, Gaston Méliès, Alice Guy-Blache and so on — encouraged by the Louisiana-born Frenchman Jules Brulatour and the French producing companies.

and the Englishmen Chaplin and Blackton were exceptions. But by the beginning of the Thirties the many accents of Hollywood were proverbial.

The first flood of foreign product after the war frightened Hollywood back into the sense of insecurity and inferiority that had, for generations, led America to import her culture from the old world. In the rush to buy up European talents, producers made bad bargains and good ones. There were inevitable but no less regrettable casualties among the immigrants; but at the same time the American cinema by and large was immeasurably enriched by its absorption of alien blood.

The principal influx of talent came from Germany where, given powerful official encouragement, the cinema had enjoyed a startling renaissance in the early years of peace. In particular *The Cabinet of Dr. Caligari* (1919) attracted international attention. For Americans (who did not in fact see the film until 1921) its use of the film for subjective and interior perceptions, the manipulation of the screen image — sets and lights and actors — as plastic material no less controllable than the painter's media, the sheer power of the film over the sensations was electrifying. Other German successes followed in bewildering succession: the inventive costume pieces of Lubitsch and Buchowetzki (in fact an *émigré* from the Russian cinema); *The Golem*, *Variety*, *The Last Laugh* (which achieved one of the special ambitions of art film makers of the day in dispensing with titles), *Faust*, *Metropolis*, *Siegfried*, *Waxworks*, *The Joyless Street*. The intellectuals in Hollywood and (more important as far as the prestige of the cinema as a whole was concerned) outside went crazy over the German films. Lewis Jacobs quotes a sub-title from Will Rogers' *The Ropin' Fool*: "If you think this picture's no good, I'll put on a beard and say it was made in Germany. Then you'll call it art." This was as early as 1922.

The first of the Germans to arrive was **ERNST LUBITSCH**, who was to be the most successful and most enduring of the invaders of the Twenties. The most influential, too: the "inimitable Lubitsch touch" was in fact imitated on all sides, and particularly in the Thirties his work had a lasting effect upon screen comedy. Born in Berlin, he had begun his career as an actor. It was while working with Reinhardt's company (from 1911 to 1918) that he starred as a Jewish comedian in a series of comic shorts which he also wrote and, eventually, directed. Against his will he was persuaded by Paul Davidson of U.F.A. to direct two dramatic vehicles for Davidson's favourite, Pola Negri: *Die Augen der Mumie Ma* (1918) and *Carmen* (1919). The super-spectacle was by this time in vogue; and *Carmen* led Lubitsch on to *Madame Dubarry* (1919), which established a new fashion for a "psychologically" realistic re-creation of history. Lubitsch pursued his own formula through *Anna Boleyn* (1920) and *Das Weib des Pharao* (1921). He was pre-eminently versatile however, and at the same time as he was making these grandiose pageants, he was developing a kind of operetta film, with *Die Puppe* (1919) and *Die Austernprinzessin* (1919), the first film in which he satirised American manners. He made screen versions of *Rausch* and *Miss Julie*; an adaptation of Reinhardt's fantasy-spectacle *Sumurun*; a rather odd and unsuccessful satire, with Pola Negri, *Die Bergkatze*, and a film in the currently fashionable "street" idiom, *Die Flamme* (1923). Between 1915 and *Das Milliardensouper*, his last German picture, he had made something like three dozen films.

Ironically, it was his flamboyant historical spectacles that spread his fame to America (where he was known as the European Griffith); and when he was brought to the States it was by Mary Pickford who wanted him to direct her in *Dorothy Vernon of Haddon Hall.* It is interesting that American xenophobia was still vigorous against directors of foreign — but particularly German — origin. Miss Pickford recalls ". . . for many at that time he was still the 'Hun', and I soon found myself being denounced as a traitor for ignoring our own directors in favour of the erstwhile enemy." These were not Pickford's only troubles. Having previously committed himself to do her picture, on arrival Lubitsch refused absolutely. Instead they agreed to make *Rosita* in which Mary Pickford failed disastrously to convert herself into a sophisticated Lubitsch heroine. The result, she said, was "the worst picture, bar none, that I ever made" but a recent festival revival was a great success. *Dorothy Vernon* was directed by Marshall Neilan.

This initial reverse — in part brought about by Lubitsch's imperfect English and his ignorance of American production methods — was immediately succeeded by the enormous success of *The Marriage Circle* (1924), based on L. Schmidt's *Nur ein Traum*, and written by Hans Kraly, Lubitsch's scenarist since *Komtesse Doddy* (1917). With tremendous accuracy Lubitsch sensed the moral mood of American audiences. He perceived the American psychology with the clarity of an outsider; he recognised the tone of the new morality, the current attitudes towards sex. Although *A Woman of Paris* can to a degree be seen as an inspiration for the direction of Lubitsch's work in America, there was a profound difference in the approach to sex of Lubitsch and Chaplin. *A Woman of Paris* worked (at least to judge from the plot) because Chaplin took sex seriously. Lubitsch introduced American audiences to a new, sophisticated, frivolous attitude to sex. Pre-war ideas of sex as the expression of deep sentiment and sacred passion were abandoned. With Lubitsch it was a pastime.

Lubitsch moreover introduced a visual form of wit that had never been experienced before in the American cinema. The actors he used — Florence Vidor, Monte Blue, Adolphe Menjou, Ronald Colman — developed means much more subtle and supple than the general equipment of screen actors at that period; they learned to use gesture and facial expression with the same sort of tact and humour with which he used pictorial detail. What is most surprising when one comes to analyse the plot of *The Marriage Circle* is how very elaborate a narrative Lubitsch was able to convey with purely pictorial means and a minimum of sub-titles. Contemporary critics were, for instance, astonished by "a scene in which Professor Stock calls on Franz Braun with the proof that he has stayed for some hours with his wife, and with a straw hat that he has left behind. The entire conversation, Franz's dismay, Stock's delight and phlegm, is pictorially perfect and lucid without a single sub-title. . . ."

The story is about two couples: the marital relations of Josef and Mizzi are strained; Charlotte and Franz are extremely happy together. Mizzi tries to seduce Franz's affections and Josef almost makes him a co-respondent in his divorce. The confusions are put right; the happy couple are happily reconciled; and Mizzi goes off in a car with another admirer. The reviewer already quoted thought the film "brilliant, subtle and at the same time satirical with a touch that can only be described as a twentieth-century Boccaccio." Lubitsch, he said "leads you up to a situation which seems as if it is going to be thoroughly banal, and then by a clever and entirely unmechanical twist avoids the obvious and achieves something entirely unsuspected. There is nothing obviously novel about the technique, but it is a crystallisation and concentration of accepted standards." This reviewer, who further added that Lubitsch had wedded "the best of American acting and German technique", had exactly recognised Lubitsch's contribution which was to be the inspiration for a whole generation of directors: Mal St. Clair, Monta Bell, Henry d'Abbadie d'Arrast, Frank Tuttle and others.

Three Women (1924) was a comedy of manners, a merciless dissection of three silly women: a mother who wanted to stay as young as her daughters and the daughters themselves — one a gold-digger, the other an idiot. Pauline Frederick's performance as the mother was very much admired; her daughters were played by May McAvoy and Marie Prevost, who before her association with Lubtisch was playing in slapstick comedy. The film appears to have been rather less successful than Lubitsch's other comedies of the period, perhaps because audiences were puzzled by Lubitsch's mixing of moods — his introduction of melodramatic and tragic elements (one of the women is tried for murder in the course of the plot) into comedy.

In his next film Lubitsch combined his success with sophisticated comedy with his experience with costume drama. *Forbidden Paradise* (1924) was an adaptation of an old stage hit by Doris Keane and dealt with the amours of Catherine the Great. Lubitsch used an actress from his German days, Pola Negri, whose success in America had until this film been limited; and playing against her as the Lord Chamberlain who alone understands the Tsarina's foibles, his favourite American actor, Adolphe Menjou. Lubitsch synthesised every element of his success: luscious sets and costumes, a flair for telling detail, a witty sexuality. Among the best remembered scenes is that in which Menjou faces a horde of revolutionaries. He reaches into his hip-pocket, as if for a pistol, but draws out a cheque book, which effectively quells the rising.

Kiss Me Again (1925) returned to modern sexual comedy. It is a triangle situation worked out with fairly familiar stage devices and situations. It is interesting to notice how at this time and to an extent throughout his career Lubitsch characteristically sought non-American settings for his sexual comedies. Indeed, not until *Design for Living* (1933) did he make a truly American sex comedy. Perhaps he felt that American men and women were not really suitable material for his sophisticated methods. Whatever the reason *The Marriage Circle* was set in Vienna, *Kiss Me Again* and *So This is Paris* in Paris, and *Lady Windermere's Fan* (1925), of course, in London. The last film, in which Lubitsch attempted to convey Wilde's comedy in purely visual terms, without making use of any of the playwright's epigrams in the subtitles, appears to have been a rather peculiar *tour-de-force*. Theodore Huff thought that "the smugness of British society was ingeniously pointed up by the attitudes of the various characters."

So This is Paris (1926) was based on a minor Meilhac and Halévy play, *Reveillon*, again dealing with the marital confusions of two married couples. The most celebrated sequence of this unjustly neglected film was the montage of a dance contest in a cabaret. The film marks one of the earliest appearances of Myrna Loy, in the supporting role of a maid.

Lubitsch next moved from Warners to M-G-M to make *The Student Prince* (1928) with Novarro and Shearer for Irving G. Thalberg. Respect for the producer's wife seems somewhat to have inhibited Lubitsch and restrained his "touch"; and the film was re-cut after Lubitsch had finished what proved a long chore and moved on to Paramount. The romantic love scenes which were interpolated (they were directed by John Stahl) were not at all in the Lubitsch tradition.

At Paramount Lubitsch returned to costume spectacle with *The Patriot* (1928). Emil Jannings, another of Lubitsch's actors in German days, played the mad Tsar Paul I in his heaviest ham style. The film was nevertheless a big prestige success. Sternberg, however, called it "*Scheisse*", to Lubitsch's lasting irritation. The production was not helped by the addition of a synchronised soundtrack of small imagination and less taste. Lubitsch's last silent film — fortunately, perhaps, overlooked in the changeover from silent films to talkies — was said to be a disaster. *Eternal Love* (1929) was a sloppy love story of the Napoleonic period, set in Austria. Again Lubitsch was ill-served by a notable actor; John Barrymore is said to have played excruciatingly badly. Lubitsch's greatest successes were yet to come.

FRIEDRICH WILHELM MURNAU was brought to Hollywood by William Fox principally on the strength of *The Last Laugh*. Hollywood was at its hungriest for European culture and art at that moment; and the florid pretensions of the Fox publicity department alienated many normally perceptive critics, blinding them to the undoubted qualities of Murnau's most important film in America. Paul Rotha, for example, called *Sunrise* (1927) "a masterpiece of bluff, insincerity, insubstantial nonsense". This is at once to underestimate the intrinsic merit of the film and to overlook the confidence that Murnau's sometimes arrogant conviction of the artistic validity of the cinema gave to American directors at a time when the film industry was most in need of this kind of reassurance. On the very eve of talking pictures, wrote Lewis Jacobs, Murnau "awoke in American producers a realisation of the boundless opportunities yet to be investigated in the silent film. His own deep personal interest and constant groping for new forms of expression, as much as his films, stimulated others to a new respect for the medium."

Sunrise was written by Carl Mayer, who had worked with Murnau in Germany and was the author of *The Last Laugh*. It is a somewhat edulcorated version of a Sudermann story: the idyll of a country boy and girl which is shattered when the boy is so seduced by an urban vamp that he contemplates murdering his wife. In the original story the boy is drowned. In the Fox-Murnau-Mayer version the young couple are reunited and the vamp goes back to the city. The subject is less important however than the style. In some ways this American film was the apogee of the German Expressionist cinema. The designs of Rochus Gliese and the superb photography by Charles Rosher evoke an atmosphere no less distinct and haunting than Murnau's *Nosferatu* had done. Even today (or perhaps especially today when we have forgotten William Fox's artistic aspirations and a degree of nostalgia enhances our view) the mists on the dawn marshes, the reflecting pavements of the rain-drenched city, the lights of the fairground, the tram-ride from country into town (this extraordinary scene was entirely shot on built stages) are bewitching. Right at the end of the silent period Murnau (who profoundly distrusted talkies) demonstrated the full scope of the silent film. In *Sunrise* he uses a subjective camera with surprising ease and fluidity. He made a film that was completely expressive without titles. (The film in fact has titles, though these were apparently inserted against the wishes of Murnau.)

The effects were not produced easily or cheaply; and William Fox must have had cause to regret the freedom he had given this distinguished foreign artist. On *Sunrise* Murnau expended tremendous pains and huge sums of money. He kept crowds of extras waiting on the payroll while the rainstorm and duststorm were mechanised. He had Rosher out in Arrowhead Lake morning after morning trying to film the sunrise which was, symbolically, to close the film; and the shot was finally faked in the studio. He built vast *trompe-l'oeil* sets for the tram-ride sequence. He transplanted a gigantic tree and then employed gangs of Mexicans to stick new leaves on it. When the leaves withered under the arc lights he had them replaced one by one. To give George O'Brien the gorilla-like walk Murnau demanded, he had his boots weighted with twenty pounds of lead. When some of the deep-focus effects Murnau required proved to be outside the possibilities of Rosher's equipment in a scene in which people had to be seen in the distant background, Murnau hired a lot of dwarfs as extras, so as to trick the perspective. In such respects as these, *Sunrise* was perhaps the most elaborate production of the Twenties in Hollywood. Even the film city was astonished at Murnau's extravagance.

His next film was, perforce, more modest. *Four Devils* was adapted from a story by Herman Bang, again by Carl Mayer. This was a heavily symbolic circus melodrama, with a *femme fatale*, and Murnau compromised with the studio so far as to give the film a happy ending. Subsequently, however, Fox tacked on a still more foolish ending with spoken dialogue. Despite this the film had a fair commercial success, but a very different critical reception from that of *Sunrise* which, for all the attacks it suffered from such dedicated cineastes as Rotha, earned Murnau the title of "the greatest director in the world" from Robert Sherwood.

Murnau's last film for Fox was also released only in a mutilated version with talking sequences for which the director was not responsible. *Our Daily Bread* (1929; released as *City Girl* in 1930) was intended as an epic of our daily food, "a 'woodcut' of life in the Dakota grain fields, showing the customs of the farmers, their backgrounds and traditions, with wheat as a symbol." Murnau, still splendidly dictatorial in the face of Hollywood producers, snapping angrily at the hands that by now rather unwillingly fed him, insisted that the film must be shot on the actual locations in Dakota; and people who saw the film praised its documentary and pictorial values. Fox grew worried, however, forced gag writers on Murnau to interpolate "comic relief", and hated Murnau's rough-cut. It is hard to imagine how much the finished film had any relation to Murnau's original conception. The plot reveals it as a melodrama about a country boy who marries a town girl and dramatic misunderstandings with the boy's farmer father which are righted conveniently at the end. At best it seems to exist in a remarkable isolation from the realities of farming existence in America in the late Twenties.

Understandably Murnau broke his Fox contract, and a little unexpectedly formed a partnership with Robert J. Flaherty, another director whose relations with Fox had ended less happily than they began. They planned a whole series of films to be made in happy independence, exploring remote corners of the world. Their first venture was *Tabu*. (Murnau had always wanted to return to the South Seas

F. W. Murnau's SUNRISE (1929), which demonstrated the full scope of the silent film.

Lillian Gish and Lars Hanson in Victor Sjöström's THE WIND (1928), the director's American masterpiece in which a young girl is destroyed by alien circumstances.

Barbara Kent and Glenn Tryon posing for an "auto photo" in LONESOME (1928), in which the Hungarian director Paul Fejos brilliantly evoked impressions of urban loneliness.

Thomas Ince, major force i shaping th American cinem of the war an post-war years

where he had fallen in love with a young man named Walter Spies; and had often asked U.F.A. to make a film there.) Financial difficulties were aggravated by a division of opinion over the story. Murnau wanted to build up the melodramatic plot about the tabu which precipitates tragedy when a young man falls in love with a girl consecrated to the gods. Flaherty had set his mind on a story about pearl-fishers. (The idea that the dispute was between Murnau's sense of the dramatic and Flaherty's ethnographic integrity hardly holds water. Flaherty, whatever his other admirable qualities, was never a stickler for anthropological accuracy.) Murnau, staking everything he owned, bought out Flaherty's interest in the picture and finished it himself, though Flaherty, as well as the cameraman Floyd Crosby, contributed to the photography. The film, released by Paramount with a banal but evocative musical score by Hugo Reisenfeld, had a world-wide success and brought profits of over $150,000 to the Murnau estate. The film still bears seeing; the images are wonderful and the drama is still oddly touching.

The tabu seemed in a strange way to cling to all those concerned with the film. Flaherty's subsequent career was dogged with frustrations. Murnau himself died a week before the preview of *Tabu*. Salka Viertel had found a chauffeur for his Packard, but he complained that the man was ugly, and selected a beautiful young Filipino instead. The young man showed off his driving; the car hit a lorry; Murnau was killed; and with him Hollywood lost one of its most potentially interesting importations.

The director of *Variety*, Ewald Andreas Dupont was brought to Hollywood about the same time as Murnau, but his single American picture *Love Me and the World is Mine* (released by Universal in 1928) appears to have been so bad that he returned rapidly to Europe, where he had somewhat more success, though even his Elstree films, *Moulin Rouge*, *Piccadilly* and *Atlantic* were not sufficient to convince his critics that *Variety* had not been the flash-in-the-pan result of a happy collaboration. Certainly it must have owed very much to the supervisor, **ERICH POMMER**, whose record as a producer can hardly be matched. Essentially a business man rather than an artist, he went into the film business in Gaumont's Berlin office in 1908. In 1915 he established Decla; and an astonishing number of the great German pictures of the Twenties were his productions, including *Caligari*, *The Last Laugh*, *Tartuffe* and *Metropolis*. In the sound era he was to be equally successful; starting with *The Blue Angel* and *Congress Dances*, Pommer, whether working in Britain, America or Germany, hardly ever knew a flop. After World War Two he again became a leading figure in the West German cinema.

Pommer's incursion into Twenties Hollywood was brief but characteristically successful. As a supervising producer at Paramount he co-scripted and nursed Stiller's *Hotel Imperial* and the intriguing but now lost film begun by Stiller but completed by Rowland V. Lee, *Barbed Wire*, from a Hall Caine novel. Pommer did not outstay his welcome. By 1928 he was back in Germany and had already produced *Spione* and *Heimkehr* for U.F.A.

In Germany **PAUL LENI** had worked at first as a designer before his curiosity and his expressionist tendencies had led him to the cinema as a film director. It was a result of the success of *Waxworks* that Laemmle invited him to Hollywood. His best film there was *The Cat and the Canary* (1927) a comedy melodrama that bore comparison with *Waxworks* and with Murnau's German horror films. Laemmle, understandably pleased with the result, commissioned three more films in the same vein: *The Chinese Parrot* (1927), *The Man Who Laughs* (1928), and *The Last Warning* (1929). Seen today, the last of these at least retains a good deal of its charm; the horror effects produced by the elaborate lighting and careful *mise en scène* are set off by pleasant comedy which compensates for the fading of the dramatic force of the film. It would be intriguing to see his last film for Universal, *Puzzles* (1929), an all-synchronised avant-garde experiment. Leni's early death cut short one of the most promising immigrant careers.

LUDWIG BERGER, a natural cosmopolitan, came to America in 1928 and worked quite happily and efficiently in Hollywood for three or four years. He directed Jannings in *The Sins of the Fathers* (1928) and Chevalier in *The Playboy of Paris* (1930), made a colour film of *The Vagabond King* (also 1930), with three other lesser works in between, and then went back to Germany, later to work in France, England and Holland.

Apart from ideas and directors and writers (Hans Kraly continued to work into the Forties; and in the Twenties wrote *The Eagle* and *The Kiss* as well as the Lubitsch successes) the German cinema enriched the Hollywood screen with new and exciting faces. Emil Jannings's Hollywood career was brief, but Pola Negri, Conrad Veidt and Josef Schildkraut enjoyed lasting success in America.

Hungarian by birth, the remarkable **MICHAEL CURTIZ** made his name in Austria where he directed a number of spectacular films for Sascha (*Sodom und Gomorrha*, 1922; *Samson und Dalila*, 1923). His international reputation was established by *Moon of Israel* (1924), a co-production between Sascha and the English firm of Stoll; and on the strength of it Curtiz was invited to America. He was bewilderingly prolific. Between 1926 and *Noah's Ark* (1929), a spectacular silent film with synchronised sound, he made nine films. None of them has been seen for many years, and none seems to have been of any real significance except in so far as they look forward to the great years of Curtiz's flamboyant talent, in the Thirties and Forties.

ALEXANDER KORDA (Sandor Korda) had also worked in Vienna and Berlin (where his best-known work was *Eine moderne Dubarry*) before arriving in Hollywood in 1927 to make *The Private Life of Helen of Troy* starring his wife Maria Corda and adapted from a story by John Erskine in the currently popular mode of humanising history. In this Korda revealed a particular flair for bringing earlier epochs to life through clever superimposition of modern psychological responses and for a characteristic blending of myth and history. Korda's main career was, of course, to be in England: none of his other American films from this period — *The Stolen Bride* (1927), *The Yellow Lily* (1928), *The Night Watch* (1928), *Love and the Devil* (1929), *The Squall* (1929), and five sound pictures — was particularly notable.

Another countryman of Curtiz and Korda, **PAUL FEJOS**, came to

America in rather odd circumstances. Trained in medicine, he worked for several years as a film director in Budapest before coming to the U.S.A. to work in the bacteriological section of the Rockefeller Institution. The stage attracted him, however, and he joined the Theatre Guild for Molnar's *Glass Slipper* (1924). In Los Angeles in 1927 he was offered 5,000 dollars by one Edward M. Spitz to make an experimental film within 28 days. *The Last Moment* was an evocation of the life of a suicide. Photographed with startling brilliance by Leon Shamroy it starred Georgia Hale, Chaplin's leading lady in *The Gold Rush*. On the strength of this film Fejos was given a contract by Universal for whom he made the enchanting *Lonesome* (1928). Two rather lonely young people meet by chance, go to Luna Park, and are separated again by the crowds. Both heartbroken at having lost their first romantic partner, they suddenly discover that they live in the next room to each other. Often endearingly funny, the film nevertheless brilliantly evokes impressions of urban loneliness. It is delightfully acted by Glenn Tryon and Barbara Kent, and today is fascinating for its precocious and extremely able use of hand-held camera techniques. Fejos made two more silent films in Hollywood (*Broadway*, 1929; *The Last Performance*, 1929) and French and German versions of George Hill's *The Big House*; then returned to Europe. When he came back to America at the end of the Thirties it was to devote himself definitively to science, as an anthropologist — an interest which is revealing in the light of the mastery of his most memorable American film, *Lonesome*.

★ ★ ★

Sweden had quite a different tradition from that of Germany to offer to the American film. In the years immediately before and during the war, Swedish film-makers had achieved a far greater maturity in their use of the medium than those of any other cinema. They attempted themes of far greater sophistication and took their cameras outside the confines of painted studio sets (a limitation which the German experience only encouraged). Working like this in natural locations had imposed further qualities: a lyrical sense hitherto unknown in the cinema; a feeling for the drama of the setting itself, for man seen against the background of a nature with which his relation could acquire a mystical quality; a restraint and realism in the acting of players, divorced from the context and associations of painted canvas scenery.

There were various reasons for the direction the Swedish cinema had taken: the influences of a particular school of Swedish literature, but particularly of the novelist Selma Lagerlöf; the ready availability of natural scenery and natural light of peculiarly photogenic qualities; the individual tastes and tendencies of the first generation pioneers — men like the producer Charles Magnusson, the cameraman Julius Jaenzon, the director Carl Engdahl.

The two greatest directors of the Swedish cinema both began their careers in the theatre. **VICTOR SJÖSTRÖM** was recruited to Svenska Bio as an actor in 1912; **MAURITZ STILLER** joined the company a year earlier. Sjöström's first film appearance as an actor was in a Stiller film, *Vampyren.* After some uncertain beginnings his first notable success as a director was an adaptation of a play, *Ingeborg Holm* (1913). In 1916 he adapted an Ibsen poem, *Terje Vigen*; and this, with *The Girl From Stormycroft* (1917) and *The Outlaw and His Wife* (1917) marked the beginning of Sjöström's most creative years. *The Girl From Stormycroft* was adapted from Selma Lagerlöf who inspired three of Sjöström's best subsequent films: *The Sons of Ingmar* (1918), *Karin Ingmarsdotter* (1919) and *The Phantom Carriage* (or *Thy Soul Shall Bear Witness*, 1920). In 1919 (with *Hans nads testamente*) Sjöström began a fruitful collaboration with the writer Hjalmar Bergman, who worked briefly with him in America in 1923.

In the course of a decade with Svenska Bio Sjöström and Stiller had each completed something like three dozen films. On his first assignment for Magnusson (*Mor och dotter*, 1912) Stiller was writer, director and actor. During the next six or seven years he established himself as a director of wide interests, but principally as a creator of witty and sophisticated social comedy. In 1919 however he first tackled a Selma Lagerlöf novel; and his reputation outside Sweden has subsequently been based — with a certain injustice — upon his series of epic films on Lagerlöf subjects: *Herr Arnes pengar* (1919), *Gunnar Hedes Saga* (1922) and *Gösta Berlings Saga* (1923-24), in which Stiller first revealed the beauty and quality of Garbo. Stiller was the terror of his actors, from whom he demanded — and won — great restraint and sensitivity. Jannings enthusiastically called him "the Stanislavski of the cinema".

Of the two directors, Sjöström was the first to come to America*, perhaps impelled as much by foreknowledge of the economic crisis about to be produced in the Swedish cinema by American competition, as by Louis B. Mayer's extravagant offer to him. Although Sjöström suffered the usual initial problems of *émigré* directors, and although his simple and noble style was not altogether in tune with the tastes of the time, he enjoyed a fair success in Hollywood — perhaps because of his policy in early American days of undertaking comparatively cheap films in which he could retain a fair degree of independence.

His first American film *Name the Man* (1923), adapted from Hall Caine, is now forgotten; but the success of *He Who Gets Slapped* (1924) is affirmed by the number of parodies that appeared within a few weeks of its release. Sennett made *He Who Gets Smacked*, Jimmy Aubrey made *He Who Gets Crowned*, and Earl Hind *He Who Gets Socked*. Adapted from an Andreyev play and starring Lon Chaney, it was a circus story which provided opportunities for Sjöström's characteristic lyricism. *Confessions of a Queen* (1925) was based on Daudet's *Kings in Exile*; but for his next American film, *The Tower of Lies* (1925), Sjöström returned to Selma Lagerlöf (the novel, *The Emperor of Portugallia*). Again his star was Lon Chaney (a favourite with the Swedish colony, it seemed; he was one of Garbo's first American friends) together with Norma Shearer. A contemporary reviewer found the film interesting "for its preservation of the simplicity of treatment notable in *Thy Soul Shall Bear Witness* and for the successful rendering of a faithful Swedish atmosphere in an American studio and with an ordinary American studio cast."

*He had actually been brought up in the United States.

In Lillian Gish Sjöström found his ideal actress. *The Scarlet Letter* (1926) was her suggestion: "I wanted to make a film of *The Scarlet Letter* and play Hester Prynne, but Mr. Mayer told me that the book was banned for the screen. I said: 'Mr. Mayer, this cannot be. It's an American classic, taught in all our schools.' Anyway, we applied for permission to make the film, and it was granted on the sole condition that Lillian Gish and no-one else played the leading role.

"I was asked which director I would like, and I chose Victor Sjöström (actually in America Sjöström was known as Seastrom), who had arrived at M-G-M some years earlier from Sweden. I felt that the Swedes were closer to the feeling of the New England puritans than modern Americans, and that even though it is an American book, Mr. Sjöström was more suitable than any of our own directors. I always considered it a great privilege to work with Mr. Sjöström.

"It was Mr. Sjöström's idea, of course, to use Lars Hanson in the part of the priest. He is a wonderful actor. We used to improvise our spoken lines before the camera, of course, and Lars Hanson's speech from the scaffold was so eloquent and affecting that we were all tremendously moved by it."

On another occasion Miss Gish wrote with characteristic perception: "His direction was a great education for me. In a sense I went through the Swedish school of acting. I had got rather close to the Italian school in Italy. . . . The Italian school is one of elaboration; the Swedish is one of repression."

Again Sjöström was able to exercise his power for lyricism and his feeling for landscape. Two years later he was able to work again with Gish on *The Wind*, a film unjustly neglected, and Sjöström's American masterpiece. (The contemporary neglect of this film was perhaps less due to the changeover to sound than to M-G-M's loss of interest in Lillian Gish after Garbo's arrival: Louise Brooks who was filming at Paramount while Sjöström was making *The Wind* at M-G-M says she never heard a word about its being made.) The theme was extraordinary: the destruction of a sensitive young girl brought about by alien circumstances. Alone and homeless, the heroine comes from the

East to live with an unsympathetic family in the West, conditioned by the hard circumstances of existence there. She feels herself forced into marriage with a coarse cowhand — a sexual union which frightens and repels her. Finally panic and terror madden her and she commits murder. Throughout it is the elements — specifically the wind — that seem to condition as well as to symbolise human emotions, that seem to mould people's lives. Magnificently photographed by John Arnold, the film captures the atmosphere of the prairie — the dust, the wind, the bright, threatening skies. (Much of the film was shot on location in the Mojave region.) Sjöström's use of visual imagery in *The Wind* to illuminate the psychology of his characters has never been adequately studied.

Between *The Scarlet Letter* and *The Wind* two Sjöström films were released. *Masks of the Devil* (1928), adapted by Frances Marion from a Jakob Wassermann novel, has not been seen since its first release, and appears to have been negligible. Garbo asked for Sjöström as director on *The Divine Woman* (1928) in which Lars Hanson was re-united with his co-star from *Gösta Berling*. Though both Sjöström and his compatriot actors were extremely happy working together the results were disappointing. The story — originally a play based on the life of Bernhardt — was debased to sentimental rubbish about a shop-girl and a soldier in the course of eight re-writes demanded by Irving Thalberg. It was a financial success but a disappointment to Sjöström. After *The Wind* and one talkie — a fashionable drawing room comedy from a Sidney Howard play, *A Lady to Love* (1930), he sailed back to Sweden.

Stiller was altogether less fortunate. The myth is that Louis B. Mayer was so impressed by *Gösta Berling* that he wooed Stiller to M-G-M and unwillingly took Stiller's discovery and *protégée*, Greta Garbo, as part of the bargain. In fact the opposite seems to be true. Garbo herself was unenthusiastic about America, since she would have preferred to stay in Berlin and work with Pabst. Louise Brooks dismisses this as the most ridiculous of the Garbo myths, pointing out that Stiller never finished a single picture for Metro. "Knowing his temper, the studio let him play interpreter and assistant director for his find until, engulfed with rage, he settled his contract and fled." Mayer and Stiller "hated each other from the day they met — Stiller because he knew Mayer viewed his work with indifference, Mayer because of the coarse indignities Stiller inflicted upon his majesty. As for Garbo's salary; in 1925, any time an untried actress got more than $300 a week the studio was really yearning for her. And nobody seems to remember how, after her arrival, Mayer kept Garbo in isolation in New York for three months trying unsuccessfully to force her to substitute a new contract for the Berlin agreement which would not hold up in American courts."

Stiller's Hollywood career was short and sad. Garbo insisted he direct her second film *The Temptress*, an adaptation from a novel by Ibañez. The idea was first suggested by Stiller himself and accepted by Mayer and Thalberg (since Ibañez was a currently fashionable writer); but Stiller's treatment was badly mauled by the Metro script department. Stiller's disagreements with the leading man, Antonio Moreno, led to Moreno's refusing to play while Stiller remained on the film; and it was completed by Fred Niblo. M-G-M and Stiller were mutually content to part company when Erich Pommer invited the director to go to Paramount, where he made *Hotel Imperial* (1927). This film remains a distinguished piece of work, strongly atmospheric and with a well controlled narrative (the story is about a servant in an hotel in Galicia, in 1915, who is caught up in the war and emotionally involved with an Austrian officer). It is an unusually handsome production and exceptional in that it was made on a huge composite set, with an arrangement of overhead rails on which the camera could move freely from area to area of the hotel and its rooms. It was a method which Hollywood did not emulate to any extent until many years later. The star was Pola Negri, with whom Stiller worked again in *The Woman on Trial* (1927), adapted from Ernest Wajda's play *Confession*. The film had a fair commercial success, but no copy seems to have survived; and reliable critical assessments are hard to find. In 1928 Stiller began *The Street of Sin*, from a scenario which von Sternberg had written for

Jannings but which, after his difficulties with the star on *The Last Command*, he did not feel willing to direct himself. Stiller did not finish the film. Halfway through he quarrelled with Paramount over some reshooting they asked him to do; and he returned to Sweden. He may already have been ill at this time. Not long after his return he died.

Another Scandinavian director, the Dane, **BENJAMIN CHRISTENSEN** (Christianson in the States) enjoyed a brief, successful and totally unexpected career in Hollywood. Christensen had a singularly capricious career. He was in turn medical student, opera singer, actor, wine merchant. In 1912 he started to write films; in 1913 he became a successful film actor; and in 1915 he began to direct. His greatest success was *Witchcraft Through the Ages* (1922), made in Sweden, which led to a contract with U.F.A. In Germany he played in Dreyer's *Mikhaïl* and directed three films of his own. Then in 1926 he went to Hollywood where he wrote and directed a couple of horror films for M-G-M — *The Devil's Circus* (1926) and *Mockery* (1927). For Richard Rowland and First National he made a further horror picture, *The Hawk's Nest* (1927), and then, characteristically unpredictable, he shot three comedy mysteries for the same producer: *The Haunted House* (1928, with Chester Conklin), *The House of Horror* (1929) and *Seven Footprints to Satan* (1929). Thereupon Christensen returned to Denmark and made no films for a decade. At sixty he resumed his career with some success.

No Scandinavian director, in fact, settled permanently in the American cinema. Nor did Sweden's finest film actor of the period Lars Hanson, achieve stardom, though his appearances in American films did not lack distinction. But Scandinavia had given Hollywood one priceless gift — Garbo.

★ ★ ★

France, which before the World War had often influenced the course of the American film (Méliès, the mystery serials, the *films d'art*) had rather less direct effect upon Hollywood in the Twenties — though inevitably the work of the avant-garde of the Twenties cannot have passed unnoticed among the younger directors. (James Cruze's *Beggar on Horseback* is the only film that suggests direct influence.) The sole French director of real distinction to come to America during these years was the Belgian-born **JACQUES FEYDER**. Brought to Hollywood by M-G-M in 1928, he remained there until 1932. Like most of the European talents rushed to Hollywood, he experienced constant frustration of his projects and only completed three original features — *The Kiss* (1928), *Daybreak* (1931) and *Son of India* (1931). In addition however he made a number of foreign versions of Hollywood successes. Thus he directed Garbo in the German version of *Anna Christie*; and made French versions of two films directed by Lionel Barrymore — *The Unholy Night* (*Le Spectre Vert*) and *His Glorious Night* (*Si l'Empereur savait ça*). He also made the German version of the latter film, which was based on Molnar's *Olympia*. *The Kiss*, scripted by Hans Kraly, was essentially novelette, a *crime passionel* trial drama, but given a degree of elegance by Feyder's *mise en scène* and his sensitive handling of Garbo and the young Lew Ayres.

* * *

Hollywood still possesses a dwindling colony of Russian character actors from the exodus of 1917 and after; but the American cinema gained few directors (Ratoff, Litvak and Mamoulian only entered the cinema after arrival in the States) and little artistic influence; for the pre-Revolutionary cinema of Russia was established on artistic and commercial bases very similar to the contemporary American cinema — an industry formed on principles of big business; an art very firmly built on literary and theatrical concepts of narrative. One of the most celebrated Russian directors, Viatcheslav Tourjansky, who continued to make films in France into the 1960s, made one film in Hollywood, *The Adventurer* (1928). Richard Boleslavski, who was Polish by birth, did not commence his Hollywood activity until after the arrival of talking pictures. Dmitri Buchowetski arrived via Berlin, where all his cinema activity had been centred (*The Brothers Karamazoff*, *Othello*, *Peter der*

Grosse, *Danton*). His American films created less impact. He made seven films in Hollywood including *The Crown of Lies* (1926) with Negri, *Graustark* (1925) with Norma Talmadge, and *Valencia* (1926) with Mae Murray. He was replaced on *Love* (1928), the first Garbo version of *Anna Karenina* and with the coming of sound returned to Germany. The great Mosjoukine, following on his spectacular successes in France, came to America. It was disastrous. His pale romantic features somehow reminded American filmgoers of Larry Semon; and after *Surrender* (1927, directed by Edward Sloman for Universal) he returned to Europe and a declining career.

The Soviet cinema, as distinct from the Russian, had much to teach the rest of the world; and the influence upon the American cinema of the works of the enchanted Twenties — of Eisenstein, Kuleshov, Pudovkin, Dovzhenko, Kozintsev, Trauberg, Yutkevitch — though indirect (for Hollywood was unable to buy up talent from the U.S.S.R. as it had done from Western Europe) was profound. Oddly enough, despite America's perennial Red Scares, the Soviet films seem to have circulated in the States much more freely than in England, where the Film Society's showings of the now classic Soviet films, around 1930, led to riots, protests and questions in the House of Commons.

The principal personal contact with the dazzling new Soviet cinema came in 1929-30 when a small but striking delegation consisting of Eisenstein, Alexandrov and Tissé arrived in America on an extended tour, ostensibly to study sound film technique. In Hollywood the trio, reinforced by Ivor Montagu, were signed by Paramount, but two scenarios — for *Sutter's Gold* and *An American Tragedy* — came to nothing. Thereupon Upton Sinclair proposed a project for a film to be made by Eisenstein in Mexico. The outcome of that — the growing discord between Sinclair and Eisenstein which ended in his refusal to let Eisenstein have the hundreds of thousands of feet of film he had shot into his hands to edit it — is one of the cinema's great tragedies.

5. Creative Producers

AFTER GRIFFITH, the two men who individually contributed most to shaping the specific image of the American cinema in the war and post-war years were Ince and Sennett. **THOMAS HARPER INCE** was the second of three sons of reasonably unsuccessful show people, and was himself put on to the stage at six years old. His youth was spent acting and in occasional attempts at promotion in which (surprisingly, in view of his later gifts for publicity) he proved unsuccessful. In 1910, hard up, he took a job with the I.M.P. company as an actor. He moved to Biograph after a few weeks, but returned to I.M.P. where the chances of directing seemed better. The first film he directed was a one-reeler, *Little Nell's Tobacco* (1910). Carl Laemmle was persuaded to make Ince a full-time director after sitting through the film with Ince by his side enthusiastically pointing out its merits. Ince directed a number of pictures, including several with Mary Pickford, before Laemmle sent him with a crew on an ill-fated expedition to Cuba, to make a series of films out of reach of the Patents Trust agents. In 1911 Ince went to the West Coast for Kessel and Bauman's N.Y.M.P. company.

Ince was inspired with the characteristically grandiose idea of hiring the entire Miller Brothers' 101 Ranch Wild West Show, for $2,500 a week, and leasing 18,000 acres of land to shoot Westerns. Ince's development of the tightly written scenario appears to have been an attempt to keep some check on one of his more ungovernable early directors, John Ford's brother Frank. (John Ford has recently said "Ince had a great influence on films, for he tried to make them move.")

By 1913 Ince's studio was turning out an average of three films a week. "Each of these little films had a definite story-line; clear characterisations; spectacular action; good production values; and clear sharp photography" (George Mitchell, *Films in Review*, October 1960). In 1913 Mutual released Ince's first feature production, *The Battle of Gettysburg*, which is believed to be the only feature actually directed by Ince himself. Running to four reels, and costing fifty thousand dollars, this was one of the great spectacle productions of its day. Among American directors who learned their craft wholly or partly under Ince were Fred Niblo, Henry King, Jerome Storm, Irvin V. Willat, John Griffith Wray, Roy William Neill, Rowland V. Lee and Frank Borzage. At Inceville too, which gradually became a great museum complex of Western scenes and properties, a whole school of cameramen was developed.

In 1915 Ince, with Griffith and Sennett, became one of the production heads of Triangle and in the same year built a big new studio in Culver City. (Culver, a developer, presented the real estate gratis.) In 1916 he produced (and claimed director credit for) *Civilisation*, which seems actually to have been directed by Raymond B. West, Reginald Barker, V. Parker Reade, Irvin Willat and other Ince directors. A great allegory in support of Wilsonian pacifism, made at a cost of 100,000 dollars, this was evidently Ince's answer to *Intolerance*.

Towards the end of the war, Ince broke with Triangle and contracted to produce for Zukor's Paramount Artcraft, starting with a rapid and successful series of war-time topicals directed by all his star directors. Meanwhile Ince's studios were continuing to produce the phenomenally successful series of William Hart Westerns directed by Lambert Hillyer. After a quarrel with Zukor, Ince released his films through Metro, until he joined in the formation of Associated Producers Inc., an organisation set up by a group of prominent producers and directors to release their own pictures. In September 1922 this organisation was merged with First National.

Although in 1921 the City of Los Angeles presented Ince with a golden key, in recognition of his services to the film industry, his post-war films no longer seemed to be in the forefront of Hollywood production. The output of the Ince Studios was as prolific as ever, but few of the films of the period after 1920 were memorable. Rowland V. Lee made *The Cup of Life*, a re-make of a 1915 title. Lambert Hillyer made *Skin Deep* and *Those Who Dance*, an early gangster film starring Blanche Sweet and Bessie Love. Ralph Ince directed Charles Ray in

Dynamite Smith. But the most successful Ince director at this period was **JOHN GRIFFITH WRAY**. His *Human Wreckage* (1922) was based on an idea by the widow of Wallace Reid and had sequences which showed the subjective vision of a drug-crazed man. He made the first *Anna Christie*, with Blanche Sweet in the title role; and *Ten Ton Love* (1924), which included a massive flood sequence in which a circus of animals is washed away, was a fittingly spectacular close to the career of Ince as producer. Ince died suddenly following a party cruise on William Randolph Hearst's yacht, in 1924.

The vanity which made Ince claim the achievements of others as his own has perhaps permanently obscured his true role in the history of the cinema. It is clear however that he was a brilliant creative producer. He knew a good film and could doctor a bad one. "He was one of the first to perceive that screen drama must consist of vivid, flashy incidents, hurrying restlessly on to a final and cumulative crisis." (John B. Richie, quoted in *Films in Review*, October 1960.) This discovery, and his introduction of the firmly conceived scenario, contributed greatly to the development of narrative *form*, as Griffith had contributed to narrative *method*. Ince himself felt that he had learned from his stage experience to judge audience reaction and audience wishes. The observations on the role of the director, already quoted, reveal a sophisticated appreciation of the film medium.

★ ★ ★

The importance of **MACK SENNETT** lay in a great body of films rather than any individual works, in a genre rather than a principle of film-making: and the films and the genre were far too gay and beguiling for anyone — least of all Sennett — to perceive that they were perhaps Hollywood's most memorable contribution to twentieth century folk lore, that they would survive in all their outrageous, irreverent and unique vitality long after films which deliberately laid claim to art had died.

Born of Irish immigrant parents in Canada, Sennett joined Biograph as an actor in 1908, and took pains to study the working principles of

Griffith. In 1909 he tried his hands at selling scenarios and provided Griffith with the story of *The Lonely Villa*. After a couple of years he began to direct, his first film apparently being *Comrades* (1911) in which he also acted.

According to Sennett himself, he conned a couple of creditor bookmakers, Kessell and Bauman, by means of some kind of Irish economics, to set him up in production in lieu of settlement of gambling debts owing by him. Keystone opened its doors in 1912 and began the enthusiastic production of comedy films which would make its name a synonym for a particular kind of slapstick comedy. In 1915 Keystone became a producing entity within Triangle. Meanwhile Sennett productions had become more ambitious, running to two and three reels in length and hanging the slapstick around stronger story skeletons.

In 1917 Sennett left Triangle for Paramount; then released successively through Associated Producers, First National, and, after 1923, through Pathe. In 1914 and 1916 he had produced a couple of features — *Tillie's Punctured Romance* and *A Submarine Pirate*. After the war he produced and in some cases directed a dozen more feature-length pictures, of which the most successful was *Mickey* (1918), starring his most brilliant comedienne, Mabel Normand, for whom Sennett had a romantic attachment which survived the star's marriage (to Lew Cody), her decline into sickness and failure, and early death. But Sennett's fame and fortune were built on his short two- and three-reelers of the vintage years.

Sennett's original stars, besides Normand, were Ford Sterling and Fred Mace, but the company was built up until there was a whole army of half-mad idiots and clowns of genius loose upon the Sennett lot. He found his actors anywhere — in burlesque, vaudeville, circuses or building sites. In 1913 he lured the none too willing Charlie Chaplin from Fred Karno's company, then touring in America. Sennett turned out stars whose different images are engraved on the folk memory of the whole world — Roscoe Fatty Arbuckle, Langdon, Chester Conklin, Charles Murray, Al St. John, Ben Turpin, Billy Bevan, Louise

Gloria Swanson in Allan Dwan's MANHANDLED (1924), a good-humoured treatment of the misunderstandings of a young couple.

The first of Cecil B. DeMille's mammoth spectacles was THE TEN COMMANDMENTS (1923) which linked Biblical times with a melodramatic modern story.

James Murray in THE CROWD (1928), King Vidor's revolutionary film which shattered the dreams of the Coolidge era in telling the story of a humble clerk's wretched circumstances.

A King Vidor film in a lighter vein: SHOW PEOPLE (1928), with William Haines and Marion Davies.

Fazenda, Marie Prevost; and others who achieved later distinction in dramatic films, like Swanson, Wallace Beery or Phyllis Haver.

The directors who emerged from the Sennett lot (they included Mal St. Clair, and Capra, both of whom worked as Sennett gagmen, and Chaplin himself) experienced a gruelling but profitable training. Sennett may have learned his craft from Griffith, but from his first comedies of 1912 he made his own clear contribution to the development of film technique. Comedy demanded a new approach to editing. The dignified proscenium set-ups favoured by drama directors in 1912, were no good to the comedians, who had to be caught where they fell. The camera had to be agile; the editing had to keep up with the jokes. Not only in America, but in Europe as well directors were astonished and stimulated by the speed and rhythm and balance of the Keystone comedies. The work of such a director as Maurice Tourneur, who came to America in 1914, reveals a sophisticated style of cutting which had almost certainly been learnt not from Griffith, but from Sennett.

The Sennett artists worked, apparently, under conditions of enviable pioneer freedom, watched over by Sennett from a tower he had built at the centre of his studio so that he could see everything that was going on at every moment. Scripts, if they existed at all, were scribbles. Improvisation and inspiration were what mattered; and invention was only stimulated by the determination of every artist to outshine his fellows in foolishness or dexterity or risk. Comics threw themselves off buildings, ran, jumped, crashed cars and got hit with mallets and run over by trains (with few serious results: the one known isolated fatal accident, it is said, did not show in the finished picture). James Agee has described the "wild man" that Sennett is said to have employed to stimulate his gagmen — "an all but brainless, speechless man, scarcely able to communicate his idea; but he had a totally uninhibited imagination. He might say nothing for an hour; then he'd mutter 'You take . . .' and all the relatively rational others would shut up and wait. 'You take this cloud . . .' he would get out, sketching vague shapes in the air. Often he could get no further; but thanks to some kind of thought-transference, saner men would take this cloud and make something of it." ("Comedy's Greatest Era", in *Life*, September 3rd, 1949).

The Keystone comedies developed a whole new comic vocabulary, deriving either consciously or unconsciously from such varied traditions as comic-strip cartoons, vaudeville and every other tradition of comic popular theatre back to ancient days. The Keystone films range from a comedy that is truly surrealist to an inspired transmutation of the life and times of the Twenties into brilliant satirical caricature. At all times their irreverence was, in the great tradition of comedy, directed at the bringing down of dignity and the undermining of authority. Was ever authority so effectively slaughtered as in the self-absorbed idiocy of the Keystone Kops?

The titles alone are cause for joy, and reveal the several sides of Keystone. There is the enchanted nonsense of *Love and Rubbish*, *Love and Doughnuts*, *Little Robinson Corkscrew*, *Love's Sweet Piffle*, *Whispering Whiskers*, *A Dozen Socks*. Or commentaries upon modern life and society, like *A Friend and Brewer* and *Home Brew*, both made in 1920; or *Lizzies of the Field* or *Tee For Two*. Best of all, and most wholesome for Hollywood morale, were the Sennett parodies of popular film successes of the time: *Down on the Sea in Shoes* (1923), *Flickering Youth*, *East of the Water Plug*, *Three Foolish Weeks*, *The Luck of the Foolish*, *Riders of the Purple Cows*, *The Sea Squawk*, *The Marriage Circus*, *The Iron Nag*, *Should Husbands Marry?* or *The Shriek of Araby*.

★ ★ ★

This is perhaps the proper place to mention **HAL ROACH**, after Sennett the most important comedy producer of the Twenties. (In the Thirties his success would actually overtake that of Sennett.) An adventurous youth had inevitably brought him to prospecting for gold in Alaska and acting in pictures; and at Universal he met Harold Lloyd. In 1915 he invested a small inheritance in establishing a film company to produce a series of comedies starring Lloyd in his character of "Willie Work". Lloyd then went to Keystone, but (to Sennett's lasting chagrin) did not succeed there and returned to Roach to make his "Lonesome Luke" series. The success of these films enabled Roach to expand his activities and in 1920 to build new studios at Culver City. His output of two-reelers throughout the Twenties was immense. Apart from Lloyd (who stayed with him until 1923) he made comedies with Will Rogers, Snub Pollard and Charley Chase. From 1922 Roach produced the *Our Gang* series; and for a brief period the eccentric Dippy-Doo-Dads comedies, played entirely by animals.

6. Recruitment

IN DEALING WITH the careers of a selection of representative directors of the Twenties — some, like King, Vidor, Capra, artists of the first rank; others reliable journeymen craftsmen; the rest ranging in a spectrum between — the most revealing method seems to be to consider them in the chronological order of their debuts as cinema directors. Interesting patterns at once emerge. There is for instance the striking recruitment of new directors in the years 1914-1916, when practically all those directors who were to shape the look of the Twenties made their first films. Again there is the changing provenance of debutant directors. The overwhelming majority of those who made their first films before 1918 had come from the other side of the camera — starting as actors, more often than not in the old New York Biograph studios where they had picked up the rudiments of their craft from watching Griffith at work. After the war, the cinema began to attract young men from a much wider range of backgrounds — brought from university, or diverted from the professions, and often tending to intellectual and literary interests that were to fit them for work in talking pictures better, often, than the intuitive approach of their senior colleagues.

1911: ALLAN DWAN

Allan Dwan was one of the most prolific directors in the history of the American cinema. In the year of his debut, 1911, he made eight feature films, and in the following year fifteen. At the age of seventy he was still turning out four feature films a year, though by this time his years of glory were past, and he was mostly engaged on second feature Westerns.

Born in Toronto, he was — despite a degree in electro-technology — irresistibly drawn to the theatre. In 1911 he had a script accepted by Essanay, and soon afterwards began to direct. At Triangle he was able to study Griffith technique, and to direct some of the early films of Pickford (*The Girl of Yesterday*) and Fairbanks. Dwan's star rose with Fairbanks: their early films together were those which showed Fairbanks as a hustling young contemporary — *The Habit of Happiness*, *Manhattan Madness*, *A Modern Musketeer*, *Mr. Fix It*; but Dwan turned with equal facility to the big Fairbanks costume films like *Robin Hood* (1922) and *The Iron Mask* (1929).

Dwan's most appealing work, however, is to be found in the series of films he made with Gloria Swanson and which dealt good humouredly with recognisable human situations, set generally in a small-town and working class or bourgeois milieu. *Manhandled* (1924) for instance is about the misunderstandings of a young couple who are temporarily separated when the boy goes to town to try to sell a new carburettor he has invented. *Stage Struck* is a no less enchanting comedy about a little waitress who has troubles with her boy friend, who cannot resist actresses. In order to compete with rival attractions, the waitress takes a correspondence course in acting, with predictably catastrophic results. Had the over-prolific Dwan's reputation depended exclusively upon these films, it might have stood higher in retrospect.

1912: BRENON, EMERSON, RALPH INCE

Herbert Brenon was another Hollywood veteran of remarkable durability. Starting work with Laemmle's I.M.P. company in 1911 or

1912, he continued to direct films in Britain until as late as 1940. Like many of the directors of his generation, Brenon came to the cinema via the theatre. Born in Dublin, he had arrived in America at sixteen to work as an actor, and had first been recruited to the movies in this capacity. He was given his chance to direct in 1915.

Brenon might have been a more memorable director had he not been early saddled with the reputation of being a director of "big films". In the war period he had made the Annette Kellerman water spectaculars and three portentous politico-philosophical pieces — *War Brides*, with Nazimova, *The Fall of the Romanoffs*, and *Invasion of Britain.* Characteristic of his later big commercial pictures were *The Garden of Allah* (1921), *The Spanish Dancer* (1923) and *Beau Geste* (1926). Surprisingly, in 1926 we find Brenon directing a version of *The Great Gatsby*. Yet his inclination was always towards subjects of more retiring charm, and particularly adaptations of sentimental stage plays. His most characteristic films now seem to be *Passing of the Third Floor Back* (1918), and his two Barrie films, *Peter Pan* (1925) and *A Kiss for Cinderella* (1926).

Brenon was also responsible for one of the most unexpected of the social comedies in which the Roaring Twenties reflected its own image. *Dancing Mothers* (1926) invests the New Morality with an altogether unfamiliar aspect of pathos and near tragedy. It is the story of a woman who, having devoted her whole life to being a good wife and mother, decides to try to keep up with her gadding husband and daughter, who have merely scorned her loyalty and affection as "old-fashioned". She discovers that her husband is unfaithful, and herself contracts a romantic liaison with the man with whom her daughter is in love. The final scenes are strikingly ambivalent in their tone, as the mother, now wooed by both husband and lover, rejects them both and leaves her home — for what?

John Emerson was practically twenty years older than the majority of directors who made their mark in and on the Twenties. Educated in Heidelberg and Chicago, he was originally intended for the church, but at the age of thirty or more he decided instead to become an actor. He was stage manager for Mrs. Fiske, and stage director for the Shuberts and Charles Frohman before joining the American Film Company, for whom he directed his first picture in 1912 (*Geronimo's Last Raid*). After the war he was mostly concerned with writing and production; his historical importance in this period lies largely in the direction which Emerson and his wife Anita Loos gave to the career of Douglas Fairbanks.

It was about this time that Thomas Ince's two brothers, Ralph and John, began to direct. Both remained active throughout the silent period; but it seemed characteristic of all three Inces that they were too deeply committed to the tastes and the times of their youth to leave any but the faintest imprint upon the films of the Twenties. In 1917 Ralph and John had attempted to establish a studio, but they met with considerably less success than Thomas Ince's production enterprises.

1913: HILLYER, CABANNE, DEMILLE

Lambert Hillyer was an Ince director who proved more adaptable to changing times, and continues to direct with moderate success. His work in the Twenties is most notable for the powerful visual sense he brought to the Western and for his revival of the flagging career of William S. Hart.

The best work of William Christy Cabanne was done in his first year or so as a director, although he continued to direct films practically to the time of his death. Entering the cinema in 1910, he was one of Griffith's assistants at Biograph. He was responsible for the debuts of Lillian and Dorothy Gish, and directed Fairbanks's first films *The Lamb* (1915) and *Double Trouble* (1915). *The Slacker* (1917) was a much-admired sentimental war film, but many films he directed in the course of the Twenties seem to have been generally undistinguished commercial chores, following prevailing fashions of the times.

The paradox of Cecil Blount DeMille was that the man who to such a significant extent shaped the image of the 1920s was essentially a

Victorian. Every one of his films was in one way or another in a direct line of descent from the theatre of Belasco, the apogee of a nineteenth century dramatic tradition. (DeMille himself, his father and his brother all at one time or another worked with Belasco.) And his work was founded upon a duality of values that was again wholly Victorian: the irresistible urge to succeed combined with a comforting, if preposterous certainty of his own concept of God and the Christian ethic.

DeMille's father died when he was a child. In 1900, at the age of nineteen, he began to act; in 1906 he began to write plays. In 1912 DeMille went into partnership with Jesse Lasky and Sam Goldfish (later Goldwyn) and went to Hollywood to direct their first — phenomenally successful — production, *The Squaw Man* (1913). DeMille threw himself energetically into production, always favouring adaptations from the stage which he knew so well. But he was a notable innovator. He did much to establish the pattern of feature-length films. He attracted notable stage players like Fannie Ward and the opera star Geraldine Farrar into films. Some of his early films use lighting effects and artificial illuminants with surprising experimentalism.

But DeMille's great gift was his intuitive ability to gauge and anticipate public taste. His war-time films — *Joan the Woman*, *The Little American* and *Till I Come Back to You* — brilliantly reflected changing public moods. And in 1918 he anticipated the new moral climate with *Old Wives For New*. DeMille claimed that the subject had been forced on him by the New York office of the organisation. Nevertheless it was a significant start to the entire cycle of socio-sexual comedies that occupied DeMille over the next few years. It incidentally contained the first DeMille bathroom scene — even though it was not in fact an exotic bathroom, but a sleazy suburban office.

The basic formula of these films, and of their countless imitators, was to predicate a modern (as of the Twenties) marriage; to show it threatened by some modern failing in one of the partners; to show the other partner driven in consequence to the consolation of another man or woman; and to show the marital breach eventually healed by the reform of the offending fault. For instance in *Old Wives For New* the wife is slovenly; in *Why Change Your Wife* (1920) she is a prim and virtuous woman whose attempts to impose her own high standards on her husband drive him to another and more attractive woman. Other films in the same series were *Don't Change Your Husband* (1919), *Forbidden Fruit* (1921), *The Affairs of Anatol* (1921, vaguely adapted from Schnitzler), *Fool's Paradise* (1921) and *Saturday Night* (1922). In *Manslaughter* (1922) and *Adam's Rib* (1922) DeMille offered his views on the flapper.

Outside the series of social dramas and comedies were *For Better, For Worse* (1921) which, despite the suggestion of its title, was not another marital problem picture but a slightly belated defence of the man who stayed at home during the war, risking insult and the white feather in order to do a job of national importance. *Something to Think About* (1922) revealed another aspect of DeMille's temperament. A piece of mawkish religious sentiment, he described it as being about "a lame man's frustrated and embittered but finally victorious search for love". In fairness it should be pointed out that the scenario was conceived especially for one of DeMille's favourite male stars, Elliott Dexter, who had emerged from a long illness with a leg disability. DeMille's adaptation of *The Admirable Crichton*, *Male and Female* (1920), brought Barrie strikingly up to date and into line with DeMille preoccupations. The emphasis of the story was altered so that its message was now essentially the supremacy of sex over class barriers. The intimate and spicy adventures of the couple, projecting everyone's wish-dreams of solitude with the loved one on a desert island, was in the outcome distinctly more DeMille than Barrie.

DeMille's films were, indeed, all the wish-dreams of the Twenties. They depicted lives of luxury and leisure, of moral freedom. More practically, they offered people examples of "how to go on", instructed audiences in contemporary manners and etiquette. DeMille shaped, as much as he reflected the life of the Twenties, from the bath tub to the dinner table.

Then, however, DeMille's career took a different turn, as a result of the unconventional means he adopted to select the theme of his next film. The studio arranged a competition in association with the *Los Angeles Times*, offering a thousand dollar prize for the best idea for a picture. DeMille was struck by the number that suggested a religious theme; and the result was *The Ten Commandments*. With his faithful scenarist Jeanie Macpherson, DeMille concocted a scenario which linked a Biblical spectacle with a melodramatic modern story about two brothers, one of whom observes the commandments while the other breaks them, colourfully, and is in the end "himself broken by defiance of the law". Costing a million and a half dollars and striking fear into its backers, this was the first of the mammoth spectacles that were to be for ever associated with the name of DeMille. Ever afterwards the moral tone of DeMille's films was lofty, though it was never allowed to detract from display and sexuality. In condemning evil, DeMille believed in depicting sin graphically and entertainingly.

The three succeeding films — *Triumph*, *Feet of Clay* and *The Golden Bed*—were necessarily anti-climactic, though the last has an intriguingly anarchic plot: Lillian Rich is snubbed by the town aristocracy for marrying a rich candy manufacturer. To revenge herself she arranges a "candy ball" (which provided DeMille with his big set-piece). The ball proves so costly that it ruins the husband.

In 1925 DeMille broke with the Famous Players-Lasky Company, bought the Ince Studios (Thomas Ince having died mysteriously after being taken ill on W. R. Hearst's yacht) and established his own production company. After a couple of flops — *The Road to Yesterday* (1925) and *The Volga Boatman* (1926) — he made his most successful silent film, and his personal monument, *The Kings of Kings*, backed by a financier with evangelical instincts, Jeremiah Milbank. DeMille himself gives some insight into his unique ability to combine piety with richly commercial displays of sex and sadism: ". . . I decided to jolt them all out of their preconceptions with an opening scene that none of them would be expecting: a lavish party in the luxurious home of a woman of Magdala, and that beautiful courtesan surrounded by the leering, sensual faces of her admirers who taunt her because one of their number, young Judas, has evidently found the company of some wandering carpenter more interesting . . ." In the outcome, as the work proceeded, DeMille's attempt to involve Christ in this rather improbable triangle situation was overshadowed by the increasing dominance of the character of the Saviour as played by H. B. Warner; and despite the fact that DeMille's adviser on the film was Bruce Barton, the author of *The Man No-one Knows*, the film remains a direct and honourable piece of craftsmanship. Will Rogers said "There will never be a greater picture because there is no greater subject" (at which DeMille commented, nervously, ". . . but it could be spoiled by poor treatment"). John Steinbeck commented more tersely: "Saw the picture; loved the book."

DeMille's career in silent films closed disappointingly with *The Godless Girl*, a resounding failure (with some sound sequences) about a high school girl who goes from bad to worse, but is finally redeemed by gaining faith in God. Writing in 1930, on the eve of DeMille's no less floridly successful career in talking pictures, Paul Rotha called him, "a pseudo-artist with a flair for the spectacular and the tremendous; a shrewd sense of the bad taste of the lower type of the general public, to which he panders; and a fondness for the daring, vulgar, and pretentious." DeMille, identifying and feeding the dreams and aspirations of the Twenties, had made himself a being of legend, embodying for all time — with his megaphone, his breeches and riding boots, his extravagance and autocracy and sense of the grandiose — the mythical image of the Hollywood film director.

1914: TOURNEUR, NEILAN, FITZMAURICE, FRANKLIN, EDWARDS, WEBER

Maurice Tourneur was a unique figure in the early days of the silent cinema. Originally an artist, and a student of Rodin, he became an actor in Rejane's company, then worked with Antoine for several years. It was only as a result of a quarrel with Antoine that Tourneur turned to the cinema, as an actor. Very soon he began to direct for the Eclair company, and in 1914 came to America to run the Eclair studios in Tucson. (As a pacifist and conscientious objector Tourneur was only too happy to leave France at this time.) His American directorial debut dates from the same year. When World Film Company took over Eclair's American interests, Tourneur began to work for them, and by 1915 the pictorial quality of his films and the clarity and speed of his narrative had placed him securely in the ranks of America's top directors. The subtlety and the sophisticated editing of a film like *The Wishing Ring* (1914) give it the look of a film made at least ten years later.

At Artcraft Tourneur directed a couple of Mary Pickford vehicles. His stylishness, which consistently attracted such praise as *Photoplay*'s review of *Barbary Sheep* (1915): "Here is poetry, here mystery, here almost hypnotic handling of light and shade", was absolutely self-conscious. Long before practically anyone else in the American film industry, Tourneur had the conviction that the film-maker was an artist: "We are not mere photographers, we are artists. At least I hope so. We must put on the screen not literal reality, but an effect which will stimulate a mental and emotional reaction in the audience."

After the war, with the immense prestige of Griffith on the one hand, the taste for a snappy, sophisticated entertainment on the other, the restrained and often somewhat dated manner of Tourneur's films was eclipsed. His productions — *Treasure Island* (1920), *The Bait* (1920), *The Last of the Mohicans* (1920, with Clarence Brown), *The Christian* (1923), *Never the Twain Shall Meet* (1924), *Aloma of the South Seas* (1926)—were prestigious, and maintained all Tourneur's old quality, but to a new generation they seemed slow. Such of them as are now available are distinguished by ravishing camerawork. In 1926 Tourneur returned to Europe where he continued to direct until the late 1940s.

Marshall ("Mickey") Neilan was a colourful and tragic figure, who might have been a distinguished director, who made and spent millions and died in a charity hospital. He left school at 11 to help support himself and his widowed mother. Among the variety of jobs he tried, he acted a bit; but when he joined the Biograph Company in 1910 or

1911 it was as Griffith's chauffeur. However, he began to act in films for Kalem and was soon Ruth Roland's leading man. He was then recruited to Allan Dwan's American Film Company, still as an actor. When Dwan passed to Universal, Neilan played there also, but then rejoined Biograph. In 1914 he went back to Kalem and persuaded the company to allow him to direct. When the Kalem contract expired, he returned to acting and was leading man to Pickford in several pictures. In 1915 he rejoined Selig, but still alternated acting with direction, for he was a supremely attractive juvenile lead, tall, handsome, and with a ready sociability that was to contribute to his undoing.

In 1915 Blanche Sweet persuaded Goldwyn to let Neilan direct her. It marked a turning point in the career of both director and star, who later married. Next Neilan directed a series of Pickford vehicles — *Rebecca of Sunnybrook Farm* (1918), *A Little Princess* (1918), *Stella Maris* (1918), *Amarilly of Clothesline Alley* (1918), *M'liss* (1918). At 26, Neilan was being paid $125,000 a picture by Pickford, and then very often did not turn up on the set till after lunch. In quick succession he directed four films more to his taste, perhaps, than the Pickford dramas, including *Hit-the-Trail Holliday* (1918), a satire on prohibition and popular evangelism. Returning to Pickford to direct *Daddy Long Legs* (1919), he also played opposite her. After an unfortunate attempt at independent production, Neilan was persuaded to make two Anita Stewart vehicles for Mayer. After this Neilan was a ubiquitous figure in the studios, popping up in first one organisation and another, turning out films which are none of them memorable, but all revealing by flashes his flair for comedy, for satire, for sympathetic and human treatment of his characters. But this promising director was the victim of his own personality. An incorrigible playboy, he never applied himself to his craft with any seriousness. Spells of work alternated with parties that lasted for days. (Characteristically, one of his happiest working liaisons in the Twenties was with John Barrymore.) He was soon known to be unreliable. Like many other artists, he offended Louis B. Mayer. By the end of the Twenties he was a has-been, and for many years afterwards the efforts of his friends to find him small jobs in Hollywood were frustrated by his own capriciousness. It is only happy to record that at the very end of his career he made a successful comeback, in a character role in Kazan's *A Face in the Crowd* (1957).

George Fitzmaurice was trained as a painter, and there always remained a strong pictorial sense about his films, allied to his complete technical assurance and a firm grasp on commercial values. He was at his best with frankly romantic themes: *The Son of the Sheik*, with Valentino, and the films he made with Vilma Banky and Ronald Colman (*The Dark Angel*, *Night of Love*) were his best works before the Thirties. One of Fitzmaurice's more notable commercial successes in the silent period was a re-make of *The Cheat* (1923) with Pola Negri in the Fannie Ward role.

Sidney Franklin, whose career stretched from 1914 right up to the 1950s, was expert at the clean, glossy sort of production with which the M-G-M studios have always been associated. Joseph M. Schenck engaged Franklin to make a series of films with Schenck's wife, Norma Talmadge, as a result of which Franklin became known as a sympathetic director of stars. Hence his assignments to direct Pickford in *The Hoodlum* (1919) and Marion Davies in *Quality Street*. Franklin seems always to have had a strong penchant for sentimentality; and it is hard to imagine that in silent films he managed it with any less discipline and restraint than in later works like the dreadful *Waterloo Bridge*, and *The Miniver Story*, though he directed *The Good Earth*. (In 1942 he received an Oscar for his production of *Mrs. Miniver*.)

J. Gordon Edwards, after a career in the theatre, became William Fox's first director, and later production supervisor. During the war he became Theda Bara's favourite director, and was clearly fired with a taste for the exotic. He became a specialist in the spectacle film; and his grandiose *The Queen of Sheba* (1921) revived the genre, which had been somewhat discouraged by the financial debacle of *Intolerance*. Two of Edwards's last films (he died in 1925) were a portent of later developments in the international industry: both *Nero* (1922) and *The Shepherd King* (1923) were produced by Fox in Italy and with Italian and French actors.

The Twenties produced a handful of Hollywood's rare women directors. The earliest of these was Lois Weber, who had begun her series of propagandist films for birth control as early as 1914 (*Hypocrites*). The series was continued under the banner of Universal (*Where are my Children?*, *Idle Wives*) for whom she made her most celebrated (and today entirely forgotten) film *The Sensation Seekers* (1926).

1915: VIDOR, KING, BADGER, BAGGOTT, LLOYD, CROSLAND

1915 was a notable year, for it saw the Hollywood debuts of two of the most admirable talents of the Twenties, King Vidor and Henry King. Both are artists whose silent films remain so completely valid today that one regrets the more keenly the total extinction of the art at the end of the Twenties. Vidor added to a high degree of craftsmanship and a powerful sense of visual symbolism a strong, instinctive social sense and a feeling for character which he could convey to his actors. "I had always felt the impulse to use the motion picture screen as an expression of hope and faith, to make films presenting positive ideas and ideals rather than negative themes. When I have occasionally strayed from this early resolve, I have accomplished nothing but regret" (Vidor in "A Tree is a Tree").

He was film-crazed from the moment he first worked as assistant projectionist in a nickelodeon, while still a schoolboy; and he records that he carefully studied — with a firm conviction that he, too, was going to make films — the pictures that he projected some time before 1910. Soon after, in his home town of Galveston, Texas, he began making movies which he sold to the Pathé Exchange. At this period he met Edward Sedgwick and Florence Arto, who as his wife, Florence Vidor, was to become one of the most accomplished silent actresses. In 1915 the young couple trekked to Hollywood, where Vidor tried his hand at any film work that came to hand.

At Universal he directed a series of "Judge Brown" two-reelers. His first feature, a Christian Science subject was (oddly enough) financed by a consortium of ten doctors. Its success launched Vidor as a feature director. He made one more film for the doctors' consortium — a comedy called *Better Times* which introduced Zasu Pitts, whom Vidor had first noticed on a bus. Vidor now established his own studio, Vidor Village, where he made half a dozen or so modest productions before going to Metro to direct Laurette Taylor in *Peg o' my Heart*. Vidor tactfully surmounted the problems of this great but temperamental and fortyish actress as a young Irish girl. He directed her later in *Happiness*. Throughout these films he was discovering a visual language, as he described in his autobiography, seeking out images which would most appropriately express a mood or an atmosphere — the romantic tunnel of willows through which the lovers of *Bardelys the Magnificent* (1926) pass; the newspaper blowing across a country road that opened and closed *Wild Oranges* (1924).

From *Wine of Youth* (1924) all Vidor's silent films were made for M-G-M, where an early and trying experience was a collaboration with Elinor Glyn, on *His Hour* (1924). Vidor's reputation was finally and firmly established with *The Big Parade* (1925), a massive, exemplary spectacle, at the centre of which was sensitively, if also sentimentally observed the experience and suffering of one, ordinary young man. It was a noble indictment of war; and no less a great piece of *mise en scène* with Vidor using the movement of troops and vehicles in a dramatic fashion hardly attempted, even by Griffith in *The Birth of a Nation*. After this he was requested as the director of *La Bohème* by its star, Lillian Gish, whose rehearsal methods, learned from Griffith, caused the director some embarrassments; but "as the making of the film got under way we found ourselves subjected to Lillian's will." Vidor was impressed by the star's complete commitment to the role, by the terrifying realism of her death scene. One of the many M-G-M films that have not seen the light of day since their first release, this must be worth revival, for the sake of Gish alone.

After *Bardelys the Magnificent* came *The Crowd* (1928), one of the most articulate of all silent films. It was an astonishing picture to come out of Hollywood at this time, when the studios were dedicated firmly to the dreams of the Coolidge era. Here was the reverse of the coin: a little clerk, one out of millions, who marries, has two children, and hopes for the miracle that will get him out of the rut. His child dies, he goes to pieces, loses his job. The home degenerates; the marriage begins to collapse. And then, at last, he gets a wretched job. The little family goes to a vaudeville show and laughs at the comics and hopes to patch life up again, tomorrow.

Everything about the film was revolutionary. Vidor dispensed with conventional plot, conventional happy or tragic end, conventional stars. His leading man was an extra, James Murray, who gave a startlingly true to life performance, then wandered off into oblivion, to drink and an early death in the Hudson River. Harry Sharp's camerawork is equally astonishing even today. The camera moves with perfect freedom, whirling about Coney Island, rushing through crowded streets (it was actually concealed in a perambulator for these shots), or — in the often-quoted opening sequence — tilting up and up a skyscraper, selecting a single window, moving in and into the great office full of clerks at their desks, finally picking out one clerk, the hero of the film. The final scene however, the family momentarily oblivious of the past and the future as they roar with laughter at the vaudeville comedian, is in its way no less memorable.

With surprising versatility Vidor turned from *The Crowd* to direct two Marion Davies comedies. The severe and often personal supervision of W. R. Hearst made work difficult for the director, but the myth that Davies was a Susan Alexander is quite refuted by these films. In *The Patsy* (1928) and *Show People* she appears as one of the most charming and witty of the Twenties comics. In the former film, as a Cinderella younger sister plotting to get her man, she does wickedly accurate imitations of Mae Murray, Pola Negri and Lillian Gish. In *Show People*, playing an actress whose rapid rise from slapstick fall-girl to dramatic star has gone to her head, she brilliantly caricatures the affectations of Twenties divas, down to the primped lips and protruded front teeth which were *de rigueur* in glamour photographs of the time.

Henry King has had one of the longest careers in Hollywood. An

Henry King's Western THE WINNING OF BARBARA WORTH (1926) which gave Gary Cooper his first starring role, and which combined spectacle with shrewd psychological observation.

William S. Hart in his last film TUMBLEWEEDS (1925), a finely made land-rush drama directed by King Baggott.

Lon Chaney in THE UNHOLY THREE (1925), the first of a series of films he made with director Tod Browning which rank among the most extraordinary ever seen.

James Cruze's BEGGAR ON HORSEBACK (1925) displayed the director's sense of the fantastic even more than HOLLYWOOD (1922).

actor in Lubin films in 1913, he was still making big prestige pictures late into the Fifties (*Carousel*, *The Sun Also Rises*). His prolific output, his commercial success and his long career have tended to obscure the sensitivity and real artistry of his best work.

King was a juvenile lead in roadshows before he joined Lubin. After his beginnings as a film actor, King had the useful experience of working at Inceville as an assistant and as a full-fledged director. Between 1915 and 1921 he made numerous minor films, which it would be interesting to see as evidence of his development which reached maturity in *Tol'able David* (1921), King's silent masterpiece, based on a story by Joseph Hergesheimer. It is a model of classical film technique, and is quoted at length by Pudovkin as exemplifying the use of the plastic materials of the cinema. It is a masterpiece both of post-Griffith ideas of montage (for which the Soviet directors most valued it) and for the *mise en scène*: the awkward adolescent love affair, for instance, is captured in a few, brief, vivid, exactly placed scenes.

King has always had a particular fondness and a particular gift for evoking the atmosphere of rural America; and even in a Hollywood wide-screen spectacular like *Carousel* there are reminiscences of the effects that marked *Tol'able David* as one of the greatest silent pictures. Subsequently King used the same star, Richard Barthelmess, in *Sonny* (1922) and *Fury* (1923).

In 1924, following the American invasion of Europe, King went to Italy to make two films with Gish and Colman, *The White Sister* and *Romola.* Outside his familiar American atmosphere, his romanticism tended to reveal clichés of sentimentality; but in his other masterpiece of the 1920s, *Stella Dallas* (1926), the sentimentality inherent in the theme was triumphantly overborne by the depth of King's perception, and his authentic tragic sense. The majestic performance of Belle Bennett is still overwhelming today.

Had King's career ended here, his place in cinema history, alongside the ten or twelve classic names of the silent cinema, would have been secure. Instead he pursued a successful and active career, producing films of both professional quality and integrity, and always within the commercial set-up of Hollywood — his reputation as a modern director obscuring the brilliance of his work as a contemporary of Griffith and Ince. Between *Stella Dallas* and his first, somewhat tentative attempts at sound pictures, King made four more silent films of which the most notable were *The Winning of Barbara Worth* (1926), a Western which combined shrewd psychological observation with finely handled spectacle, and which marked the starring début of Gary Cooper; and *The Magic Flame*, a costume picture with an Italian setting, designed to exploit the exotic charm of Ronald Colman and Vilma Banky.

A graduate of the Sennett school, Clarence Badger is an unjustly neglected director of comedy. Such work of his as can now be seen has a verve and polish which have survived better than many more classic contemporaries. Joining Sennett in 1915 as a scenarist, he very quickly began to direct; and in 1918 made his first feature, *Friend Husband* for Goldwyn. From 1919 to 1921 he directed a long series of films with Will Rogers (*Jubilo*, *Guile of Women*, *Honest Hutch*, *The Strange Boarder*, *Boys Will Be Boys*, *An Unwilling Hero*, *Doubling for Romeo*), which were among the comedian's best, bringing out a certain pathetic quality in his cowboy characterisations.

Badger had a special talent for directing lady comics. He had directed Swanson at Sennett's, and Bebe Daniels in *Miss Brewster's Millions* (1926), *The Campus Flirt* (1926) and *Hot News* (1928). But his best comedienne was Clara Bow, whom he directed in three of her most successful films: *It* (1927), *Red Hair* (1928) and *Three Weekends* (1928) — the last apparently a parody of Elinor Glyn, who had first created the concept of *It*. *It* is a much better and more charming film than its reputation had led one to fear. The film is fast and funny, and Bow (as the shopgirl who sets her cap at the boss) a charming as well as a witty heroine. There are some notable comic scenes: Betty Lou as a saucy counter-hand, or dining at the Ritz, compensating, like Eliza Doolittle, for her lack of social know-how by the quality which Madame Glyn (who also appears in the film) defines as "It". And the speed with which the cheerful absurdity of the ending is achieved is exemplary.

Hands Up!, in which Badger worked with Raymond Griffith, a comedian whose elegance and polish matched the director's own, is a neglected classic of silent film comedy, with a logic and attack that rank with Keaton. Griffith is caught in a totally Keatonesque situation, involving Mormons, Indians and Civil War spies. Several sequences are memorable: Griffith teaching the Indians, who are about to scalp him, the Charleston; or producing plates from under his opera cloak and spinning them in the air, circus fashion, to attract the aim of the firing squad about to shoot him.

In some respects King Baggott might be regarded as the first male star. When in order to publicise his capture of the Biograph Girl (Florence Lawrence) for his own I.M.P. company, in March 1910, Carl Laemmle staged a stunt and publicised the name of Florence Lawrence, King Baggott's name was published along with hers — the first time that cinema actors had been thus identified. Baggott went with Miss Lawrence to St. Louis where they were mobbed by excited fans, and fragments of Miss Lawrence's clothing were torn off by souvenir hunters.

Baggott appeared in upwards of three hundred films, and between 1915 and 1928 directed some twenty-eight pictures. Few of these have survived; but *Tumbleweeds* (1925), William S. Hart's last film, is a beautifully made land-rush drama. The actual rush, photographed by Joseph August, is one of the cinema's great action sequences, brilliantly staged and impeccably edited. *Lovey Mary* (1926), which starred Bessie Love, was a sentimental small-town drama, admired for the restraint and dignity of its handling.

Typical of the reliable, versatile commercial directors who were as capable of surviving the upheavals of the immediate post-war cinema as the later sound revolution is Frank Lloyd. A Scot, he had worked in the English theatre and toured in Canada before playing villains in a number of Universal films, around 1913-14. He passed to direction in 1915, and shortly afterwards moved to Fox, who possibly appreciated Lloyd's sentimental tendencies on the one hand, his literary inclinations on the other. Lloyd displayed bewildering versatility in his huge output of silent films, though he seemed always drawn back to literature — Dickens for *A Tale of Two Cities* and *Bleak House*; Balzac, for *The Eternal Flame*, Raphael Sabatini for *The Sea Hawk* — for his big prestige successes.

Another debutant of 1915, Alan Crosland was a journalist, critic and actor before coming to the cinema. He managed to pursue a comparatively undistinguished career, making derivative routine commercial films, until 1926 when he leapt to celebrity as the director of the first all-synchronised film, *Don Juan* (1926), and later *The Jazz Singer* (1927). Crosland's silent work—his picturesque melodramas and his *Three Weeks* (1924)—would now, perhaps, reward reassessment.

1916: INGRAM, NIBLO, SEITZ, CRISP, ROBERTSON, SCHERTZINGER

Rex Ingram came to America from his native Dublin in 1911. He studied fine arts, and his intense interest in plastic form dominated all his films. Ingram's approach was in every respect sophisticated (in 1927 he named as the five greatest films *Intolerance*, *Potemkin*, *Chang*, *Caligari* and *A Woman of Paris*). He was always concerned that "the massing of figures, the distances, the arrangements of light and shadow, will compose something of pictorial value. . . .

"Of course," he wrote, "film presents more complicated problems than do paint or clay. Painters and sculptors can study out the effects they want, but moving picture composition changes momentarily, and a fine bit of grouping that has taken the director a long time to compose may be unbalanced in a twinkling by some changes by an actor or a group of extras.

"The film director must also be careful about form. As it is with clay and paint, form is one of a film's most vital adjuncts. Take the closeup for instance. Without a knowledge of the construction and forms of the human head, it is only by chance that the director can light it in such a way that the modelling is brought out.

"It is the modelling obtained by a judicious arrangement of lighting and shade that enables us to give something of a stereoscopic quality to the soft, mellow-tone closeups that take the place of the human voice on the screen and help to make audiences intimately acquainted with the characters" (Ingram, in "Motion Picture Classic," July, 1921; quoted in *Films in Review*, May, 1952).

Ingram's first film as director (he had acted, designed and been an assistant with Edison and Vitagraph; and been a writer at Fox) was *The Great Problem* (1916), the first of eight films he made at Universal before joining the Royal Flying Corps. After the war, and after a further brief period at Universal, he went to Metro, where his career was definitively re-launched with the triumph of *The Four Horsemen of the Apocalypse*. His subsequent films — *The Conquering Power* (1921), adapted from *Eugénie Grandet*; *The Prisoner of Zenda* (1922), *Scaramouche* (1923), *Where the Pavement Ends* (1923), *Mare Nostrum* (1926), *The Arab* (1924), *The Magician* (1926), *The Garden of Allah* (1927), *The Three Passions* (1929) — all revealed the same visual refinement, combined with the same taste for the exotic. After one last film, *Baroud* (1931), independently made in North Africa, Ingram finally retired from films. "In the old days," he said, explaining his move, "the director and cameraman put on the whole show. I had one cameraman — John F. Seitz — all the time. Today you're dominated by equipment."

Fred Niblo was a model of the conscientious, craftsmanlike, entirely professional director of the Twenties. In the 1890s he had been a vaudeville entertainer, and from 1902 to 1904 toured with The Four Cohans. A year or so later we find him returning from an extended voyage to Africa, and touring with a lantern lecture about his experiences there. Thereafter he returned to vaudeville and appeared on Broadway in Cohan shows. (As a septuagenarian Niblo returned to the stage after his Hollywood career had ended.)

In 1916 or 1917 Niblo married an Ince actress, Enid Bennett, and arrived in Inceville as a "producing director". After directing fifteen films under Ince's guidance, all starring his wife, Niblo founded his own producing company. His real success began however with his association with Fairbanks. After *The Mark of Zorro* (1920) and *The*

Three Musketeers (1921), Niblo was typed as a director of costume spectacle. He directed Valentino in *Blood and Sand*, and was given the formidable assignment of *Ben Hur* which had been begun in 1922 by Goldwyn but was eventually inherited by M-G-M who began the work all over again, at the cost of three year's work and an ultimate reputed total of six million dollars. Reaves Eason shot the chariot race, shot with forty-two cameras and a cast of a quarter of a million extras. Recalling his work with other stars (Fairbanks, Valentino, Novarro) M-G-M gave Niblo a couple of Garbo vehicles — *The Temptress* (1926), begun by Stiller, and *The Mysterious Lady* (1928) — and two ambitious films designed to star Norma Talmadge, a modern version of *Camille* (1927) and an adaptation of *Adrienne Lecouvreur*, *Dream of Love* (1928).

George B. Seitz began life as a prolific writer of romantic plays and adventure stories, with a bit of acting experience in between. In 1923 he joined Pathe as a writer, and scripted dozens of Pearl White serials. In 1916 Seitz was one of the founders of the Astra Film Corporation, which took over Pathe's New York studios and production of the Pearl White serials, which Seitz now directed. Next he opened his own studios and between a project for a serial on the life of Christ, produced seven successful serials, in some of them starring himself, as well as writing and acting. Seitz continued to direct serials — among them the very last American Pearl White — right up to the mid-Twenties.

In 1925 he began to make features with the same enthusiasm as he had brought to serials. A terrifying professional, he always turned in his film on time or ahead of schedule. Most of his silent films were Westerns which are forgotten or lost; but one deserves mention. *The Vanishing American*, adapted from a novel by Zane Gray, has as its theme revolt against the old oppression by Red Indians returning from the war of 1914-18. The last scene, the death of the Indian hero (Richard Dix), in the arms of the white girl with whom he is secretly in love (Lois Wilson), is remarkably discreet and touching.

Donald Crisp is a figure whose contribution to the silent film has been undervalued — perhaps because of the division of his work between direction and acting. Born in London and educated at Oxford, Crisp emigrated to the States in 1906 and acted and directed for a couple of years in the theatre before going to Biograph as an actor in 1908. He was Griffith's assistant on *Birth of a Nation* and *Broken Blossoms*, and in the latter film played the role of Lillian Gish's brutal father. Between 1916 and 1930 he directed numerous films, including Fairbanks's *Don Q, Son of Zorro*. He was Keaton's co-director on *The Navigator* (and his is the face in the horrible portrait which menaces Buster through a porthole). It is nevertheless as an actor that Crisp will be best remembered: his career spanned half a century, from 1908 to the end of the Fifties, and ranged with unwavering integrity from Grant in *Birth of a Nation* to the genial old paterfamilias in the *Lassie* films and the old man in *A Dog of Flanders*.

An almost totally forgotten director, despite the efforts of Lewis Jacobs to revive interest in him in "The Rise of the American Film", is John Stuart Robertson. Robertson, who joined Vitagraph as an actor in 1915 and began to direct for the same company in 1916, seemed to bring intact to the screen the honest, craftsman traditions of the turn-of-the-century theatre. (He was an actor from 1890 and played with Frohman's and Maude Adams's companies among others.) Jacobs wrote of him: "His films are marked by the sensitivity and sincerity of his cultured, quiet temperament. Called 'the best-liked director in Hollywood', he is a man of fine tastes, intelligence and dignity. . . . His task has been to salvage the sentimental and to render it with poignancy. He has been a sort of American Seastrom: his films have delicacy and refinement, are quiet and unpretentious but sincere and moving. His reticence in both his personality and his work, in an industry which believes in self-advertisement, has caused him to remain in the background. If he has been little noticed, however, he nevertheless is a distinct and valuable figure in American film history."

Robertson's first notable success was the John Barrymore *Jekyll and Hyde* in 1919. Later he directed Pickford in *Tess of the Storm Country* (1922) and Garbo in *The Single Standard* (1929), a rather improbable vehicle about a girl who demands sexual equality but finally settles for mother-love. Robertson seems to have been especially happy when working with Richard Barthelmess, whose quiet and tender style clearly suited his own temperament. With Barthelmess he made *The Bright Shawl* (1923), *Classmates* (1924) and *Soulfire* (1925).

Victor Schertzinger, whose highly successful work as a commercial director extended as late as *The Road to Singapore* (1940) was an Ince discovery. Originally a concert violinist and arranger, Ince first hired him to write scores (including one for *Civilisation*; and when he became a director after 1916 — he made most of the early Charles Ray films — his musical instincts seemed to give to his films a particular fluidity.

1917: TOD BROWNING, VAN DYKE

Improbably, Tod Browning, having run away from school to join a circus, was a vaudeville comic at the time he went into movies as an actor at the Biograph studios. He played in Griffith's *The Mother and the Law*, was one of the Master's assistants on *Intolerance* and directed his own first full-length picture in 1917. From 1918 to 1923 he directed a series of programme pictures for Universal — most of them routine melodramas though *The Virgin of Stamboul* is admirable. Between 1923 and 1925 Browning took to drink. In 1925 he was taken on by M-G-M and began the series of films with Lon Chaney that must rank among the most extraordinary pictures ever made. *The Unholy Three*, about a transvestite ventriloquist, a dwarf and a strong man who conduct a criminal business under cover of a pet store, was a promising (and profitable) beginning. After a more conventional crime film, *The Mystic* (1925), Browning and Chaney embarked on a series of seven further films — *The Blackbird* (1926), *The Road to Mandalay* (1926), *The Unknown* (1927), *London after Midnight* (1927), *The Big City* (1928), *West of Zanzibar* (1928) and *Where East is East* (1929). The premises of the films were outrageous. In *The Blackbird* Chaney plays the dual role of a crippled bishop and a crook who impersonates him. In *The Unknown* he is an armless wonder in love with Joan Crawford. In *West of Zanzibar* he is a crippled magician seeking revenge on Lionel

Barrymore. Browning, a conscientious, painstaking craftsman at all times, was possessed of a uniquely strange vision, which saw a sort of beauty in horror.

W. S. Van Dyke was another theatrical child who found his way into the movies. His father died before his birth, and he travelled about with his actress mother. As a youth he followed his mother into the acting profession, then, like Browning, became one of Griffith's six assistants on *Intolerance.* His first film was *The Land of Long Shadows* (1917). In the Thirties Van Dyke was to become one of M-G-M's most reliable and versatile directors, equal to anything from *The Thin Man* and *Andy Hardy* to *Naughty Marietta* and *Marie Antoinette.*

But Van Dyke's inclinations always took him out of doors. He started in Westerns, and frequently throughout his career came back to the horse opera. Characteristically, a flat, overdressed M-G-M glossy like *Winners of the Wilderness* (1927) comes to life the moment that Tim McCoy is loosed into the hills and forests. And apart from the *Thin Man* series the films one most readily associates with Van Dyke are out-of-doors subjects, *Trader Horn* (1931), *Tarzan of the Apes* (1932), *Eskimo* (1933). In the silent period he is chiefly remembered for the picturesque *White Shadows in the South Seas* (1928) which he took over after Flaherty's quarrel with M-G-M.

1918: JAMES CRUZE

James Cruze was, like some of his contemporaries, too prolific and facile a director for the good of his reputation. In twenty years he made upwards of a hundred films. The facility came from his long and sound apprenticeship. By 1900 he was an actor; in 1906 he was a member of Belasco's company (the lavish, spectacular and conscientious *mise en scène* of Belasco seems to have had a considerable influence on a number of early film-makers. In 1908 Cruze joined the Thanhouser company as an actor, and stayed there for several years, appearing in *She* and *Cymbeline* among other ambitious projects of the company. Moving to Lasky in 1916, it appears to have been a further two years before he directed his first feature film, *Too Many Millions* (1918).

In the next decade his rise was swift and his success enviable; but Lewis Jacobs's judgement on him in 1940 was "a cynic to whom film making was easy, Cruze seldom exerted himself to produce anything superior to what was demanded." Cruze himself, Jacobs recorded, confessed himself too anxious to please, and without "guts". His versatility was surprising. After a series of romantic comedies with Wallace Reid, he made three Arbuckle slapstick features. A fourth was adapted for Will Rogers after the Arbuckle scandal of 1922. A fantasy with elements of satire, made in the same year, *One Glorious Day* was compared, perhaps misleadingly, with *Caligari*.

The following year Cruze made his most famous film, *The Covered Wagon*. Today it is perhaps easier to divorce the commonplace story from the spectacular and documentary quality with which the struggles of the pioneers of 1850 are re-created. The scenes of the trek, the fording of the river, the division of the ways as the caravan divides, part to go to Oregon and part to California, are still inspiring. (It is worth recalling Will Rogers's clever parody of *The Covered Wagon*, *Two Wagons — Both Covered* (1923), in which the pioneers arrive in California to find the real estate profiteers awaiting them.)

Cruze was possessed of an independent sort of fantasy, almost an element of surrealism, which makes him one of the most intriguing of Twenties might-have-beens. It showed in *Hollywood* (1922), which had an altogether fantastic dream sequence, in which the hero rows through the streets of Los Angeles in a boat. Cruze cannot have been entirely "without guts", as he claimed, for the film is celebrated for its (for the times) brave reference to the Arbuckle scandal. His sense of the fantastic was carried even further in *Beggar on Horseback* (1923), from the play by Kaufman and Connelly. Made for Famous Players-Lasky — a company not noted for experimentalism — the film sounds to have had some remote relationship to the French *avant-garde*: "The camera showed people unnaturally large or small, overdressed, overjewelled, stuck to chairs. Rooms appeared absurdly large; ostentatious settings were greatly exaggerated; the courtroom scene was stylised and fantastic throughout; actors' movements and gestures were sharp and grotesque." (Jacobs).

By this time Cruze had moved on to social comedy, turning films out with startling speed: *Ruggles of Red Gap* (1923), *To the Ladies* (1923), *The Garden of Weeds* (1924), *The City that Never Sleeps* (1924), *The Enemy Sex* (1924), *Merton of the Movies* (1924), *Welcome Home* (1925), *The Goose Hangs High* (1925), *Marriage* (1926), *Waiter From the Ritz* (1926), *On to Reno* (1927), were only a few of the titles of the films of the late silent period.

But Cruze was restless. In 1927 he tried to repeat the success of *The Covered Wagon* with *Old Ironsides*, a spectacular production from a Lawrence Stallings story. Earlier, and more modestly, he had made a Western of exceptional charm, *The Pony Express*. Again there is an element of documentary reconstruction in the account of the riders of the pony express, linking the two ends of the continent. In Ricardo Cortes, Cruze discovered a hero who combined Valentinoesque good looks with a cheerful humour. An oddity of the film, which seems somehow characteristic of Cruze's ability while working at high pressure to avoid conventional clichés and stereotypes, is that the villain, played by George Bancroft, goes scot free at the end, despite his interference with the mails and his collusion with hostile Indians.

Cruze deeply mistrusted talking pictures and only worked in them unwillingly. He never again achieved the success he had known in silent films.

1919: ST. CLAIR, BORZAGE

Mal St. Clair was a newspaper cartoonist before joining Mack Sennett in 1915, first as a gagman, and after 1919 as a director (his first film was a short, *Rip and Stitch Tailors*). Sennett resisted the young man's attempts to bring greater subtlety into Keystone comedy, and in 1921 St. Clair went freelance, collaborating with Keaton on two splendid shorts, *The Goat* and *The Blacksmith*. His first feature production was *George Washington* (1923). A couple of Rin-Tin-Tin vehicles earned him the undesirable reputation of being a dog director, over which he triumphed with the brilliant *Are Parents People?* (1925), the first film St. Clair made for Famous Players-Lasky. After that he was in demand as a top director of social comedies, and worked with stars like Florence Vidor, Adolphe Menjou, Pola Negri, Tom Moore. In 1926, with his comedies, *The Grand Duchess and the Waiter* and *Woman of the World* he was at the peak of his career. That year he was voted third — after Lubitsch and Stroheim — in the list of the best American directors. Curiously, shortly afterwards St. Clair, whose skill at sophisticated comedy had equalled that of Lubitsch and *A Woman of Paris*, seemed to lose his impetus. After *Gentlemen Prefer Blondes* (1928) he essayed different genres, but never again had a big success. In the Thirties his work was mostly on second feature productions; even the features he made with Laurel and Hardy, *Jitterbugs*, *Dancing Masters*, *The Big Noise* and *The Bullfighters* turned out to be among the comedians' least successful work.

Too few of the silent films of Frank Borzage are available accurately to assess their reputation. The thick sentimentality of his later films must already have been pronounced in his early work. (His first film, made in 1919, was *Ashes of Desire*.) His most prestigious pictures of the Twenties were *Seventh Heaven* (1927) and *Street Angel* (1928) both starring the ideal romantic couple of the period, Janet Gaynor and Charles Farrell. Unseen for many years, their critical reputation varies from "poetic and tender" (Georges Sadoul) to "eyewash" (Paul Rotha). Time seems likely to favour Sadoul's view.

1920: CLARENCE BROWN, SEDGWICK, LEE, GISH

Clarence Brown is an artist of integrity and excellence quite beyond ordinary ideas of a "commercial" director which, supremely, he has always been. Trained as an engineer and originally employed in the automobile industry, he entered the cinema as assistant to Tourneur; and two of his earliest films *The Last of the Mohicans* (1920) and *The Foolish Matron* (1921) were co-directed with Tourneur, though the first film on whose credits Brown's name appeared, *The Great Redeemer* (1920) was credited to him solely as director. Responsibility for individual parts of *The Last of the Mohicans* has been disputed. A somewhat static, "picturesque" film, magnificently photographed by Philip Dubois and Charles Van Enger, it is sensitive in its handling; and the spectacular climactic struggle on the rocks is succeeded by an exceedingly touching final scene of the death and burial of the white girl and the Indian scout who have fallen in love.

Brown is supremely a romantic, but the romanticism of *The Eagle* (1925) is tempered with a light satirical humour which makes it one of the best and liveliest of all the Valentino films. The self-effacing elegance of this film — the subjection of style to story — has all the characteristics which mark Brown's pictures, right up till his most recent. In his next film, *The Goose Woman* (1925), Brown used Louise Dresser very differently from the way he handled her as the Empress in *The Eagle*. A sentimental melodrama about a *prima donna* fallen into drunken squalor, and her regeneration, it is notable for the startling and vivid naturalism of the sequence of the heroine in poverty. Dresser's memorable performance was certainly the result of Brown's talent for handling actresses. He directed Pauline Frederick in *Smouldering Fires* (1924) and Norma Talmadge in the excellent *Kiki* (1926).

But Brown's most admirable silent films were the two he made with Garbo: *Flesh and the Devil* (1927) and *A Woman of Affairs* (1928). The first was a difficult assignment, since Garbo did not like the Sudermann story which required her to play a *femme fatale*. She was however reassured by the presence in the cast of Lars Hanson, and elated by playing opposite John Gilbert, to whom she was first introduced by Brown. Brown had a genius for moments that brought out Garbo's extreme sensuousness. In one memorable scene Garbo takes communion, and turns the chalice so that her lips shall touch the same spot as her lover's have already moistened.

There is a still more magical moment in *A Woman of Affairs* where Iris March, delirious from sickness, comes out of her hospital room and picks up the flowers that her lover has left, embracing them, stroking her cheek upon them with the same intensity of sensory expression that she found again in the bedroom scene of *Queen Christina*. It had been Garbo's own idea to adapt Michael Arlen's *The Green Hat*, though the expurgations demanded by contemporary Hollywood morality emasculated it (if that is, in the circumstances, the word) and reduced it to novelette. Yet the integrity of Brown's romantic vision, coupled with the intensity of the star's performance, transcend the material. Brown was later, in the course of a prolific and entirely honourable career, to direct five of Garbo's sound films, including *Anna Christie* and *Anna Karenina*.

A busy and reliable commercial director, Edward Sedgwick came from a circus and vaudeville background ("The Five Sedgwicks"). He wrote and directed a *Fantomas* series in 1920-21, had a period as a director of Westerns with Tom Mix and Hoot Gibson (*Dead Game*, made with the latter as star in 1923, is a good-humoured and extremely efficient piece); and then established himself as a comedy director. *Tin Hats* (1926), *Slide, Kelly, Slide* (1927) and *West Point* (1928), respectively guying army life and two hallowed American institutions are well spoken of; but his reputation rests principally upon a series of Keaton films he directed during the comedian's last sad days at M-G-M, beginning with two silents, *The Cameraman* (1928) and *Spite Marriage* (1929). It was perhaps unfortunate that Sedgwick's subsequent career should have been established upon these films, which must have been very largely the creation of Keaton himself. Certainly Sedgwick — though he was to direct comics of the calibre of Joe E. Brown and Red Skelton — never equalled them again.

It is worth recalling that Lillian Gish directed a film, *Remodeling Her Husband*, scripted by Dorothy Elizabeth Carter, and starring Dorothy Gish and James Rennie. Griffith persuaded her to do it, since he "thought that men would work better for you than for me". It was a pity that Miss Gish, with her high intelligence and sensitivity, never repeated the experiment, which in this case seemed to have been simply handicapped by technical inexperience.

Among directors trained under Ince's supervision, Rowland V. Lee was distinguished by his expensive academic education. Lee's early career is slightly mysterious, but he was once described as "spending his early days between the New York Stock Exchange, the stage and the pictures". He was acting with Ince as early as 1915, served in the war and returned to Inceville in 1920, as a director. He re-made Ince's own 1915 success, *The Cup of Life* (1921); but achieved his first big success with *His Back Against the Wall* (1922). In 1923 he made the first of several versions of *Alice Adams*; and in 1927, under the supervision of Erich Pommer, he made *Barbed Wire*, a pacifist film, starring Pola Negri.

1921: HOWARD, HILL, MARION

William K. Howard was a director whose artistic aspirations never seemed fully to be realised. He joined Universal's press department, and had his first chance to direct with a rural romance, *What Love Will Do*, in 1921. Later he was typed as a director of Westerns and adventure films; and his reputation with the intellectuals of the time was established with one of these, *White Gold* (1927), in which he employed techniques of erotic and psychological suggestion derived from the German expressionists. The film's lack of commercial success probably discouraged Howard. Certainly his experimental inclinations seem to have been restrained throughout the rest of his career, whose highlights were *The Valiant* (1929), a notable pioneer sound film, *The Power and the Glory* (1933) and *Fire Over England*, made for Korda in Britain.

One of the minor lost talents of the cinema seems to have been George William Hill, whose early death cut short a talent that on the evidence of *The Big House* (1930) and the strongly characterised comedy *Min and Bill* (1930) was still developing. A stage hand at Biograph at 13, he graduated to cameraman and worked for many years in this capacity at Kalem, Triangle, Bosworth and Goldwyn, before writing and finally directing films. The best work of his brief career — *Zander the Great* (1927), *The Cossacks* (1928)—was done in collaboration with the scenarist, Frances Marion, whom Hill married. Marion herself, who was Pickford's favourite writer, directed the star in two films (also made in 1921), *The Love Light* and *Just Around the Corner*.

1922: FRANK TUTTLE

Frank Tuttle came to Paramount from Yale and *Vanity Fair* (where he was assistant editor) to become one of Hollywood's most prolific and reliable directors. Of the fast, sexy, dramatic, commercial films he made between 1922 and the sound period (he continued to direct until 1959) the best are *Lucky Devil*, *Love 'Em and Leave 'Em* (with its somewhat unappreciated performance by Louise Brooks), *Second Fiddle* and *Kid Boots*. Tuttle instituted The Film Guild, an off-shoot of The Theatre Guild.

1923: CAPRA, GOULDING, WELLMAN

Frank Capra had a switchback career in silent movies which gave little accurate prediction of his subsequent career in talking films, except in so far as he early demonstrated his independence of approach, his easy craftsmanship, the instinct for psychological probability that made his work with Harry Langdon so much more successful than any other films in which the comedian appeared.

Capra's career was a classic story of nineteenth and early twentieth century America. He arrived in the States around 1900, one of seven children of a Sicilian immigrant who earned his keep as an orange picker in California. Frank sold newspapers to help the family budget, and then worked his way through the California Institute of Technology. Graduating in 1918, he joined the army. Afterwards he drifted about until 1923, when he sold himself as a director to a new company devoted to the production of one-reel film versions of famous poems. Capra did *Fultah Fisher's Boarding House*, innovating the use of types instead of actors less out of artistic persuasion than so that there should be no pros about to recognise his inexperience.

Lawrence Gray and Betty Bronson in ARE PARENTS PEOPLE? (1925), a triumph for director Mal St. Clair.

Victor McLaglen and Louise Brooks in Howard Hawks's A GIRL IN EVERY PORT (1928), a sharp and lively comedy that was its director's best work in the silent period.

A drama directed by Charles Chaplin: Edna Purviance and Adolphe Menjou in A WOMAN OF PARIS (1923), the story of a demi-mondaine's tragedy told with considerable originality of technique.

Buster Keaton directed and starred in SHERLOCK JUNIOR (1924), a comedy which had an ingenious dream framework.

Harry Cohn hired him to make Columbia Screen Snapshots. Then Capra moved to Sennett as a gag man, where he became interested in devising a consistent comic personality to suit Harry Langdon. Sennett later recalled, "Capra wanted Langdon as soon as he set eyes on him". He saw a peculiar quality of invulnerable innocence in this weird little man who looked (as Agee said) like an elderly baby, and dressed like a baby: tiny boots on inturned feet; a squashed round hat that sits where it has been perched atop his head, turned up all round and with a half-formed kiss-curl creeping under it.

Capra wrote *Tramp, Tramp, Tramp* (1926) for him, a beautiful thing in which Harry wins a cross-country walking race, despite imprisonment, a cyclone and infatuation for Joan Crawford. *The Strong Man* (1926) was Capra's first feature as a director and is wonderfully assured in structure and handling. It opens with Harry as a World War I soldier, gleefully bombarding his enemy with ration biscuits shot from his catapult, and ends with the utter destruction of a vaudeville saloon in which Harry, standing in for the Strong Man, has become entangled in his stage equipment. The fact that at the moment the building collapses the righteous of the town are marching round the ungodly place in emulation of Joshua outside Jericho, recalls a much earlier gag which Sennett attributes to Capra and which illustrates his reliance upon providence to provide the comic *deus ex machina*. A Sennett idiot pursued by a cop pauses long enough to offer supplication. At that moment a piece of machinery falls off a passing aeroplane and brains the cop. "That," says the sub-title, "is what I call service."

Long Pants (1927) had Langdon as a small-town boy deceived by a scheming floozie. Less close-packed with invention than *The Strong Man*, it has an endearing, poetic whimsy about it which begins in the often recalled scene in which Langdon bicycles foolishly round and around the car in which the loved one sits, his pace slackening as his infatuation becomes more intense.

The Langdon films were made for First National release; and after the comedian went off to establish his own company, Capra made a routine romantic comedy for the same organisation. *For the Love of*

Mike was an unqualified disaster, sending its star, Claudette Colbert, back to the stage and practically putting Capra out of movies. He went back to Harry Cohn's Poverty Row company, Columbia, where he began a series of films which established the fortunes both of Columbia and Capra. The films were made very cheaply, with stars who for one reason or another were available at cut rates. But Capra's extreme efficiency, the independence of his approach (he attributed the failure of *For the Love of Mike* to accepting a formula picture and treating it in a formula way), his sense of comedy and instinct for character, raised the films above the "quickie" level, to compete favourably for screen time with programme pictures from M-G-M or the larger studios.

Capra's first feature for Columbia was *That Certain Thing* (1928), starring Ralph Graves and Viola Dana. Of the remaining six silent films which he directed in the same year and early 1929, *The Power of the Press* is probably the best. A fairly conventional newspaper and crime thriller, it has Douglas Fairbanks Junior as a reporter helping the daughter of an election candidate to clear herself of suspicions of implication of a murder. The film is fast and efficient (as the circumstances of its production demanded) and the playing has a delightful feeling for light comedy.

The other films in the series have been described as "topically flavoured comedy dramas, expert exercises in the laughter and tears formula" (Richard Griffith). *The Younger Generation* (1929) was based on a Fannie Hurst novel on a clogs to clogs theme. The earlier films, for cheapness's sake, were original scenarios. The plot of *The Way of the Strong*, about a crook who cannot bear the sight of his own face and falls in love with a blind girl, only to lose her, hints at the sentimentality which was always to handicap even the best of Capra's comedy. With *Submarine* (1928) and *The Donovan Affair* (1929) Capra entered the sound era.

One of the few directors to arrive in Hollywood from the British theatre was Edmund Goulding. Emigrating to America in 1915, his activity showed bewildering variety, ranging from the novel *Fury* to the hit play of the Twenties, *Dancing Daughters* (1924), from the screenplay of *Tol'able David* to the title song of *Teenage Rebel* (1956).

Goulding's debut as a director was an adaptation of his own novel *Fury* (1923: it has no relation to the Lang film of the same title). His best-remembered silent pictures are *Sally, Irene and Mary* (1925), one of the most charming and melancholy "flapper" films, starring Sally O'Neill, Joan Crawford and Constance Bennett, about the loves and tragedies of three show girls; and *Love* (1927), the first Garbo *Anna Karenina.*

Many silent directors were able to survive to a degree into the talkie period. William Wellman seemed to be one of the other kind, who only fully realised himself in talkies. After war service, he became an actor in films (*Knickerbocker Buckaroo*, 1919), and then did all manner of studio odd jobs until 1923 when he directed his first picture, *The Man Who Won*, for Fox. He made half a dozen more films for Fox, was borrowed by Columbia (at that time a fairly sure sign of failure, however temporary) for *When Husbands Flirt*, made *The Boob* for M-G-M and then settled with Famous Players-Lasky for whom he made his most famous silent films, *Wings* (1928), which, with *Lilac Time*, established the whole vogue of aviation films, and *Beggars of Life* (1928) with Louise Brooks and Wallace Beery.

1924: MONTA BELL

Monta Bell, originally an actor, had his first contact with the cinema when he collaborated with Chaplin on the comedian's account of his European visit "My Trip Abroad" (1922). The following year he was one of Chaplin's four assistants on *A Woman of Paris* and this experience, together with the example of Lubitsch, was formative to the style of his best work, social comedies like *The Snob* (1924), *Broadway After Dark* (1924), *Pretty Ladies* (1925), *The King on Main Street* (1925). Unexpectedly Metro gave Bell Garbo's first film, *The Torrent*, to direct. Garbo is said to have found him most unsympathetic, and he is credited with bellowing, "Get that big woman back here on the set."

All three of Chaplin's other assistants on *A Woman of Paris* also became directors in their own right. Edward Sutherland became an excellent comedy director, though his best work was done with W. C. Fields in the Thirties. Henri d'Abbadie d'Arrast, one of two French assistants Chaplin engaged to ensure accuracy of his French settings, made several successful and witty social comedies, including *Service for Ladies* and *A Gentleman of Paris*. Jean de Limur became a director in the early period of talkies. Earlier Chaplin associates who became directors were the English comic Albert Austin, who made a couple of films, *My Boy* (with Jackie Coogan) and *Trouble* in 1921, and Chuck Reisner, who appears as co-director with Buster Keaton on *Steamboat Bill Junior* (1928).

Another important director of comedy who made his début about this time, though his real importance only becomes clear with the advent of talkies, was Stan Laurel, a veteran of the Fred Karno variety company and of Hal Roach comedies before he accidentally teamed up with Oliver Hardy in 1927.

1925: COOPER AND SCHOEDSACK, MILESTONE, WYLER

Merian Caldwell Cooper was from childhood a natural adventurer and explorer. He left the Annapolis Academy because he preferred flying to the navy, volunteered for service against Pancho Villa, flew bombers in the First World War, fought with the Poles against the Russians, escaped from a Soviet prison camp, became a journalist and planned to be an explorer. He first worked with Ernest B. Schoedsack on a round-the-world expedition. Raising $10,000 with the help of a journalist and traveller, Marguerite Harrison, they set out to make a film about the struggle for existence of primitive man, as exemplified by remote tribesmen of Persia and their annual trek to find grass for their cattle. Jesse Lasky saw the finished film, *Grass* (1925), and financed Schoedsack and Cooper on another exploration film. This time Cooper's sense of drama — always stronger than his integrity as an anthropologist — led them to choose a jungle location in Siam. The result was the deliberately sensational *Chang* (1927).

Lewis Milestone was born in Kishmev, in the Ukraine, and after commercial studies in Europe reached America, apparently as an illegal immigrant, just before the First World War. After varied work in Hollywood, he emerged as a writer on Alan Crosland's *Bobbed Hair* (1925) and as a director on *Seven Sinners*, made later the same year. It is a pity that his comedy *Two Arabian Nights*, made for Howard Hughes, and which took an Oscar for the best direction in 1927, appears to have disappeared. *The Racket*, a gangster film with Louis Wollheim and Mary Astor, drew from Rotha the praise that the director was "well aware of the right use of half-lighting, of well-chosen camera angles, and of contrasted motives of tension with unexpected movement of material". After one more silent film, *The Garden of Eden*, Milestone came to real eminence with *All Quiet on the Western Front* (1930).

Another director of the Thirties who was serving an arduous apprenticeship in silent films was William Wyler, who had taken a job with Universal (Laemmle being a relation of his mother's) in 1920. In 1925 he began to direct a series of two-reel and feature Westerns, only escaping from this rut in 1928 when he made *Has Anybody Here Seen Kelly?*

1926: HOWARD HAWKS

The long career of Howard Hawks belongs essentially to the sound period, but his beginnings were in silent films. After a university education and training as a mechanical engineer, he improbably became a prop man on a Mary Pickford picture, then worked in the editing and script departments. For a time he was Marshall Neilan's assistant, before getting his chance to direct with a couple of comedy shorts. He wrote and directed his first feature film, *The Road to Glory* for Fox, in 1926. (He was to re-make it ten years later.) Comedy continued to interest him; the same year he made *Fig Leaves*, an intermittently successful farce, written by Hope Loring and Louis D. Lighton, which parallels the domestic problems of Adam and Eve with a contemporary couple, Adam and Eve Smith. It is a strikingly elegant film, designed by William Cameron Menzies, with costumes by Adrian, and photographed by Joe August. In 1927 he made *The Cradle Snatchers* and *Paid to Love*; and the following year he directed his best silent picture, *A Girl in Every Port*, a sharp and lively comedy about the rivalries of two amorous sailors, and starring Louise Brooks. The title of *The Air Circus* (1928) reflected Hawks's interest in aviation (he was a First World War flyer; and in 1930 directed *The Dawn Patrol*). His last silent film was *Trent's Last Case* (1929).

1927: KARL BROWN, DOROTHY ARZNER

A brilliant cameraman (he worked with Cruze on *The Covered Wagon*, *Ruggles of Red Gap* and *Beggar on Horseback*), Karl Brown, a former Griffith assistant, and Bitzer's collaborator on the photography of *Intolerance*, did not find his niche as a director and writer until talking pictures, though he made two silent films in 1927, *Stark Love*, for Paramount, and *His Dog*, for DeMille.

Dorothy Arzner was a lady director less socially committed than Lois Weber, but certainly more talented. Graduating from the University of Southern California, she became an assistant director and editor, working on *Blood and Sand* (1922) and *The Covered Wagon* (1923). After a period of writing, she directed her first film, *Fashions for Women*, in 1927; and the rest of her silent films were social comedies, now valuable as period studies of feminine psychology (*Ten Modern Commandments* and *Get Your Man*, both made in 1927; *Manhattan Cocktail*, 1928).

7. Six Masters

AMONG THE CONFUSION of Hollywood directors of the Twenties — the innovators and the hacks, the journeymen and the artists who managed to maintain their creativity uncompromised by the production lines — a half dozen figures stand out unique and apart from the rest: Chaplin, Keaton, Stroheim, Sternberg, Ford, Flaherty. It is not unreasonable to ask why Ford should be included here and not the Vidor or the King of silent days; why Keaton and not the wonderful Stan Laurel (even though Laurel's most inventive work was done in the sound period); and there is a slightly arbitrary element in the selection, and perhaps a degree of personal and period taste. One's choice of masters might be different twenty years hence; it would certainly have been different twenty years ago.

But these six have in common that every film they made is recognisable for its style and personality alone; that some way or other, to some degree or other, each found the means of creating art — personal and authoritative — in the confines of industrial Hollywood. Chaplin's unique spell upon the audiences of the whole world guaranteed him the possibility of complete independence, which he seized and maintained. Keaton, until he was crushed in the rapidly growing organisational machinery of the late silent period, was profitable enough to be supported in comparative independence by the industry. Stroheim fought a battle with Hollywood which he could only, in the long run, lose; and did lose it. Sternberg's dominating talent and flamboyant personality were tolerated by the baffled industrialists. Flaherty precariously scraped along on the edge of things, managing to complete a tiny handful of pictures according to his own taste. And John Ford, through his majestic half-century of film-making, has had the supreme happiness of finding the work which he loves and pursues with enthusiastic independence of spirit, in exact accordance with the commercial needs of the industry.

★ ★ ★

At the moment of writing, the eclipse of **CHARLES CHAPLIN**'s critical reputation is practically complete. In 1939 Lewis Jacobs devoted an entire chapter of his "The Rise of the American Film" to Chaplin alone, while writing off Keaton in a bare two lines. Two generations later, the situation is pretty much reversed, except that Chaplin might be lucky to get two lines in a contemporary history, for the feeling towards him is not simply neglect, but a more positive antagonism. The position is unjust, but not entirely inexplicable. There was bound to be a reaction against the entirely uncritical adulation which lasted from the First World War to the 1950s. The long-term effects of Chaplin's political unpopularity in America, too, were imperceptibly to infect the attitudes of those who would, consciously at least, normally resist the witch-hunting and intolerance that persecuted the man's over-simplified humanist views. Chaplin's own attitudes and attitudinising have not helped. More and more his public face has suggested lofty defensiveness on the one hand and on the other a curious respect for his own legend and a continuing fascination with his own eminence.

A more concrete factor in the critical reaction against Chaplin is a new awareness of the essential naïveté of his film-craft. Chaplin learned it at the Sennett Studios in 1914 and 1915. Achieving a brilliant mastery of film technique as it existed at that date, he never saw fit to sophisticate his style. A Chaplin film of any period is archaic in technique. By the same token, of course, his films exist in a way out of time, old-fashioned, but undated by the vogues of later years.

Finally of course Chaplin (though long may he live) has outlived himself in some respects. He is inclined to be judged on his last films, *A King in New York* and *A Countess from Hong Kong* which contain only glimmerings of his real quality, rather than on the master-works of the Twenties.

Content is pre-eminent in Chaplin's work; and the essential content is the character he created. Whatever one's other feelings about Chaplin, it is impossible to deny the potency of his tramp-clown — the one universal symbol created by the cinema in its first half-century.

By the end of the war the general lines of that character were clearly established — the range of his emotion from callousness to high sentiment, of his behaviour from the noble to the larcenous, but all conceived within a human framework which makes his encounters with elements of real life — love, religion, war, poverty, unemployment, authority, crime, children, hypocrisy, cruelty — capable of satire and criticism. The crucial elements in Chaplin's formation were his poverty-stricken childhood as the son of an improvident music hall singer and his wife, also a performer and in precarious mental condition, which brought him into contact with the life of slums and charitable institutions of Victorian London; and his own long apprenticeship on the music halls. The first experience gave his outlook a clarity, a keen and wholly realistic appreciation of the situation of the underprivileged. The music hall years sharpened his comic techniques to wonderful precision and versatility. Added to this, of course, was a native grace and rhythmic sense, a rare invention, a purely poetic instinct and (sometimes overlooked among the rest) the qualities of an impeccable actor.

With one notable exception, Chaplin's films of the post-war decade are variations on the theme of the tramp clown — the Universal Everyman — cast into different, recognisable human situations. All were produced independently by Chaplin himself, the earliest under a contract with First National to produce eight two-reelers within eighteen months for the sum of one million dollars plus a $15,000 bonus for signing, plus additional bonuses in the event of any of the films running longer than the agreed two reels. Financially this contract was not as advantageous as his previous agreement with Mutual, but it gave him new and complete freedom. The brilliance of the best of these films reveals the advantages of this independence; at the same time Chaplin was freer to indulge that sentimentality and taste for pathos which attracted so much admiration from his contemporaries and has contributed so much to the distaste of later generations.

His first film for First National release was *A Dog's Life*. The second, released three weeks before the armistice, was *Shoulder Arms*. Distilling as it does all the real horrors of war into a comic fantasy which is hard and black and essentially unsentimental, this is the most durable of all the many films made about that war. Chaplin not only demonstrated his often-repeated principle that truth is the first essential of comedy; but proved that comedy, like poetry, could be a potent distillation of truth. Neither *Sunnyside* (1919) nor *A Day's Pleasure* (1919) which followed *Shoulder Arms*, was a success, though both seem to have contained rewarding scenes. The first has Chaplin improbably on the farm; and scenes of ingenious home-made labour-saving devices sound Keatonian. The second, the trials of a family picnic outing, derive from music hall turns and presage similar films with Laurel and Hardy and W. C. Fields — particularly the scenes in which Charlie has trouble with a recalcitrant automobile.

These comparative failures were followed by Chaplin's greatest success, *The Kid* (1921). An odd mixture of rich comedy and Victorian pathos (the unmarried mother is introduced with the title "Her only sin — motherhood") it aroused tremendous enthusiasm in audiences all over the world, and grossed over two and a half million dollars for First National. Jackie Coogan became one of the most characteristic idols of the Twenties.

Inevitably *The Idle Class* (1921) and *Pay Day* (1922) were anti-climaxes after this triumph. *The Idle Class* is an over-elaborate, over-plotted affair with Chaplin in a dual role as tramp and also as alcoholic millionaire. *Pay Day*, Chaplin's last two-reeler, is unusual in giving the tramp an identifiable social station and context. He works on a building site and has a nagging wife. Nor did *The Pilgrim* (1923), a four-reel feature, repeat the success of *The Kid*, although it now appears as one of Chaplin's most sustained comedies. This time the tramp is an escaped convict who is mistaken for the new pastor of a tiny rural community. It has some sequences of very funny comedy at the expense of village aristocracy; a splendid passage with a dreadful child; and the celebrated church scene, with Chaplin's mimed sermon on the text of David and Goliath, and his professional assessment of the haul in the collection boxes.

With *The Pilgrim* Chaplin fulfilled his First National contract. Although in retrospect the films sometimes lack the vigour of, say, the earlier Mutual series — films like *Easy Street*, *The Vagabond*, *One A.M.* and the admirable *The Immigrant* — they have a new polish, the result, certainly, of the endless pains Chaplin took over his shooting and editing. No other comedian took so long over his films, and Chaplin's shooting ratios are enormously high even by today's standards.

After *The Pilgrim* Chaplin was free to release through United Artists which he had founded with Griffith, Fairbanks and Pickford in 1919. *The Gold Rush* (1925) is an elaborate episodic comedy which derives its peculiar strength from the underlying blackness of the situation. Behind the gags and laughter the theme is the privation and the jealous greed of the nineteenth-century gold prospectors. One scene, in which Mack Swain, crazed by hunger, thinks that Chaplin is a chicken, is a reminder that the inspiration for the film was the Donner party disaster whose victims appeared to have been reduced to cannibalism. Practically the whole repertory of the gags in this film have become legendary; it is one of those rare pictures whose lore has been passed down from generation to generation. Sometimes, too (as throughout his career) Chaplin has been done the disservice of flattery for inventions that were not his own. The celebrated dance of the rolls, for instance, was a routine used years before, no less skilfully than by Chaplin, by Fatty Arbuckle in *The Cook*. Blind spots in Chaplin's technique are most clearly revealed by a comparison of this film with Buster Keaton's *The Frozen North*, made three years earlier. Though the Keaton film is altogether more modest in its resources, it is interesting to note how much more appreciative Keaton is than Chaplin of the visual potential of his setting. By comparison Chaplin's is a visually uninteresting film.

By now Chaplin was expending enormous sums of money and time on his pictures. Shooting of *The Circus* (1928) was constantly interrupted by the unseemly divorce action brought by Lita Gray (until his marriage to Oona O'Neill, Chaplin's private life was always dramatic and highly publicised). Chaplin himself had no affection for the film, which is nevertheless a well-constructed comedy, with gags which, if they show no appreciable advance on the films of ten years earlier, are admirably polished.

Despite projects to play Napoleon and Christ (Chaplin was always haunted by the comedian's dream of wanting to be Hamlet) he embarked on *City Lights* almost as soon as *The Circus* was released. By this time however, sound threatened, and Chaplin halted production. He seems to have feared talking films less for their technical demands (after all he was a resourceful actor with a fine and individual voice) than because it meant the loss of an international audience. When Chaplin resumed production on the film, it was to release it as a silent film with added sound effects — a hopeless anachronism and yet an astonishing success in 1931 and on every subsequent re-issue. *City Lights* illustrates better than any of his films the timelessness that resulted from Chaplin's refusal to recognise changes and refinements in film language. The naïve directness of his story-telling, the total unreality and yet powerful ambience of the studio sets he built for the film, the admirable artifices of the film's structure, the vitality of the central tramp-character and its ability to exist right outside ordinary historical chronology, give the film the quality of fable.

There remains the film which Chaplin directed, but from which his clown character was absent — *A Woman of Paris* (1923). Reputedly suggested by a meeting with Peggy Hopkins Joyce, the novelty of the film (apart from the surprise of Chaplin's emergence as a dramatic director) was less in its story, about a demi-mondaine's tragedy, than in its treatment, which probably influenced Lubitsch and certainly made a lasting impression upon the subsequent work of Chaplin's four assistants on the film — Monta Bell, Mal St. Clair, Jean de Limur and Henri d'Abbadie d'Arrast, all of whom rapidly became directors in their own right.

People who have seen the only available copy of this film (in Moscow) express a certain disappointment; but there is no doubt that Chaplin's contemporaries found it full of innovations. These were evidently natural extensions of the techniques which Chaplin had perfected in his personal comic performance. Much of his humour had been built upon effects of allusion and suggestion; and in *A Woman of Paris* he employed the same kind of allusive quality for its dramatic effect. The reflected lights of a train substitute for the train itself. The relationship between the man and the girl is illuminated by details such as the man's collar which falls out of a drawer in the girl's apartment. Cigarettes, jewelry, chocolates, dresses equally played dramatic roles.

Chaplin evidently achieved his effects at the cost of great labour. He is said to have ordered 200 takes of one scene in *A Woman of Paris* and Adolphe Menjou described how he made something like a hundred attempts to get right a kiss which "in his case had to show passion, yet avoid any indication that he was in love; in Edna Purviance's case it had to appear that it was not repulsive to her yet to show that she was unhappy" (Theodore Huff: "Charlie Chaplin", Schuman, 1951). It is clear that this film had enough technical originality and skill in *mise en scène* to suggest that Chaplin, had he not been primarily concerned with creating a theatre for his tramp-clown character, would have been a considerable director, as well as a great performer whose universal qualities did much to enforce respect of the cinema as an art form.

★ ★ ★

While the game of comparing the relative merits of Chaplin and **BUSTER KEATON** is as vain a pursuit as the old examination riddle about Dickens having more power but Thackeray more art, it is interesting to compare the different assets that Chaplin and Keaton derived from their comparable backgrounds in music hall and vaudeville. Chaplin in his days with Karno (and earlier, literally at his mother's knee) had learned about performance and gag structure, about what constituted a valid stage character, acceptable in human terms, about how to build and pace and time a stage routine, and how to control an audience. Keaton had learned all this too in years with his family's act (he was on the stage from the age of three or four, and by his early teens he was a star in his own right) improvising and developing business under the professional guidance of his father and the hyper-critical eyes of vaudeville audiences in early twentieth-century America. But Keaton had learned other arts too. Trained from babyhood, he had developed an athleticism and agility which enabled him, as performer, to "perform miracles as easily as he breathed". He could leap or somersault, or fall off a cliff or a house-side. As an actor he had no less power than Chaplin, though he was blessed with more restraint and a finer natural taste. He had a curious mechanical gift which he brought to the structure of his films and gags, as well as to the creation of enchanting and crazy mechanised props for his pictures. Overall, from the habit of working out acts and gags, he had developed an approach to the solution of individual given problems which made him, when he came to apply it to the problems of making films, one of the most creative artist-craftsmen of his times.

"The Great Stone Face" is a groundless myth. Buster's was the most expressive face in films. Someone asked him why he never smiled, and he replied, precisely, "I had other ways of showing I was happy." A slow blink can express a climax of joy; and when, at the end of *The Three Ages* he gets the girl and celebrates by throwing his hat, quite sedately, into the air, his ecstasy is an explosion. He could not be maudlin, but there is a moment in *The Cameraman* which is as poignant as any in the cinema. The girl he loves and has just rescued has gone off with the other fellow. Buster, seen in long shot, simply sinks to his knees by the lake shore.

The pathos is only temporary, for Buster triumphs soon afterwards. And this is the key to all the characters that Keaton plays (for, unlike Chaplin, he plays different characters in each of his films). He is so small and alone and vulnerable; and yet he can never remain pathetic for long, for he is also self-reliant, indomitable, endlessly resourceful. Fate may help, but it is by his own ingenuity that he triumphs in the end over the seemingly insuperable. The characteristic Keaton plot situation confronts the unaided and strictly human hero with some vast problem and then sets him to discover the solution.

Naturally, Keaton rapidly assimilated the techniques of movie-making as they existed in 1917. (Keaton was walking along Broadway one day, and met Roscoe Arbuckle, "And he said, 'Well, come on down to the studio Monday and do a scene with me or two and see how you like it . . .' ".) His mastery lay not only in his use of camera and process tricks (he used back projection "before it was invented" and some of his tricks have never been completely explained: the multiple exposures of *Playhouse* are still unsurpassed). More important, his solution of every problem of *mise en scène* is unerringly correct. From about 1923 he can be considered the equal of any film director working in Hollywood.

He possessed too an impeccable sense of structure; gags were never simply tacked on but were germane to the narrative and a dynamic element in it. Within the gags themselves there is the same sense of structure, the same fascination with mechanical engineering. The gags of the mature films are built up as *enchaînements* of geometrical and dynamic design and beauty. The quality first emerges clearly in a sequence in *The Three Ages* (1923). Buster, escaping from a police station, climbs on a roof, springboards across a crevasse between sky-scrapers on to a ledge, falls three storeys through blind awnings, grabs a drainpipe which breaks away and propels him through a full 180° arc and into a window two floors below which proves to be the dormitory of a fire station. He slides down the fire pole on to the back of an engine just as it is driving off to a fire — which happens to be at the police station from which he has escaped. All this is in one unbroken, rhythmical, elegant movement, perfectly demonstrating Buster's impeccable timing as actor, director and editor.

Keaton's quality is seen from his very first appearance on the screen, in Arbuckle's *The Butcher Boy* (1917). His performance was shot without rehearsal or re-takes — a staggering achievement for a first camera appearance. Already it is clear what Buster brought from vaudeville, what he had to contribute to screen comedy. He does a corny gag about a quarter-piece in a tin of molasses, and the troubles that ensue when he gets molasses in his hat and treads in a sticky pool on the floor. His timing, his accuracy in planting and placing a gag, above all his restraint (the face was already fixed in its solemn dignity and the body already moved like a complex of little piston rods) are in striking contrast to the frenzied, uneconomical leaping and running and grimacing of the rest of Arbuckle's troupe. No doubt Buster's presence and success with the public exerted its own influence; at least in the year or so he was with the Arbuckle company, the frenetic pace was restrained, and there are clear signs of greater precision in building gags. Familiar Keaton jokes and gag structures begin to appear.

Even so there is a marked change in the first two-reel shorts made after Keaton left Arbuckle to form his own production company in 1920. The stories of the two-reelers are tauter, the gags begin to reveal Buster's solemnly crazy logic. In *One Week* ("only one-third as passionate as Elinor Glyn's *Three Weeks*") we have the first of Keaton's encounters with an inanimate monster: a do-it-yourself house-construction kit. Throughout the whole series of shorts, individual gags and preoccupations are seen in development. The celebrated stunt in *Steamboat Bill Jr.* (1928) in which the side of a large house collapses on Buster, who escapes by standing exactly at the spot where the open window will fall, is mooted in *Backstage* (1918) where a stage flat falls on him, and further refined in *One Week* (1920). Already at this time his co-stars included trains, boats and rivers. In *Neighbours* (1920) we first become aware of his meticulous care for realistic stagings, in the slum street that is the setting for some polished comedy routines.

The classic shorts of these early years are *Playhouse*, a triumph of trick work, with Buster playing all the players and all the audience in a vaudeville theatre, and *The Boat* (1921), the first of the great comedies of his maturity. The story of a suburban family's adventures in a home-made boat, it is a crescendo of catastrophe, from the moment that Buster in his Model T tows the "Damfino" out of the door of the cellar in which he has built it. The boat is too wide for the opening, and pulls away the foundations of the house, which collapses into a heap of rubble (to Buster's thoughtful and wide-eyed surprise). The ship is launched and slides down the slipway with Buster proud and erect in the prow . . . and down, and down until the water gently laps over Buster's still upright head.

His first feature film, directed by Herbert Blache, was *The Saphead*, adapted from a venerable stage play about an idiot who accidentally saves the family fortunes, and is chiefly interesting (apart from the opportunities it affords for some of his vaudeville acrobatic comedy) as his first encounter with the character of the rich, spoilt, simpleton to which he was to return in later films.

The first feature which Keaton directed himself was *The Three Ages*, a parody of *Intolerance*, which relates the rigours of courtship in the Stone Age, Roman times and the present day (that is, 1923). Rich in gags, it lacks the elegance of *mise en scène* which was later to be Keaton's hallmark and which is so striking in *Our Hospitality*, made in the same year. Set in the early days of the railway era, this has Buster caught up in a southern feud. A film of quite astonishing visual beauty, it contains one of Keaton's most remarkable "geometrical" gag sequences, a rescue on top of a waterfall. Harold Lloyd had nothing on Keaton when it came to dangerous and acrobatic feats without the benefit of doubles or stunt men or safety nets.

In the course of the next six years, Keaton made ten more silent features. Sometimes other directors or co-directors are credited, but there is no doubt that Keaton's conception dominated. *Sherlock Junior* (1924), with an ingenious dream framework, had Buster as a master-detective rounding up a gang of criminals. *The Navigator* (1924) takes the enchanting premise of a young millionaire couple adrift on an ocean liner, with Buster's ingenuity applied to the problem of adapting resources intended for 1,000 people to the use of two. In *Seven Chances* (1925) he is a young man who must find a bride within twenty-four hours in order to inherit a fortune. He escapes pursuit by an army of veiled Amazonian would-be brides, only to find himself caught up in a landslide.

Two films made in 1925 and 1926 betray a temporary slackening of invention, perhaps because after *Seven Chances* Keaton lost his old gag team of Clyde Bruckman, Jean Havez and Joseph Mitchell. Both

Go West and *Battling Butler* depend heavily on plot, being thin in gags and often betrayed by an unusual carelessness in staging. But whereas *Go West* is saved by its exceptional charm and a handful of very choice comic moments, *Battling Butler* after a promising start drifts into an uncharacteristic masochism in its story of a weakling's being mistaken for a prize fighter.

Keaton recovered triumphantly with *The General* (1926), still the masterpiece of silent film comedy, impeccably developed and with the pictorial qualities of Brady's Civil War. Asked why he thought his picture of the war was so much better than *Gone With The Wind*, Keaton once explained, "They went to a novel; I went to the history books." The theme of *College* (1927) resembles a Harold Lloyd story, but its comic sequences are altogether Keaton's own — Buster as a soda jerk or trying his hand at college athletics, or coxing a boat with the rudder tied to his behind. The beautiful *Steamboat Bill Junior*, in which Buster returns from college to appal his rugged steamboat captain father with his pansified ways, but proves his mettle by rescuing both his father and his sweetheart from a cyclone, was the last film which Keaton produced independently.

After 1928, Keaton's company was absorbed into M-G-M, and soon it became clear that there was no room for methods of film authorship as personal as Keaton's, whatever the results. Keaton was assigned directors; his scenarios were submitted to committees. Despite the changed climate, *The Cameraman* (1928) was a complete success, with some of the comedian's most engaging gag sequences. But *Spite Marriage* (1929) his last silent film, was uneven. It was the beginning of Keaton's decline, which accelerated when — like other great artists before and after him — Keaton offended Louis B. Mayer. Deprived of the means of his art, he spent many years in a wilderness of alcohol and enforced inactivity. Only towards the end of his life did he achieve belated recognition as the supreme artist that he was, whether as clown or film-maker.

★ ★ ★

ERICH VON STROHEIM's war with Hollywood lasted longer, and the battles were more bitter. Von Stroheim was born in Vienna, the son of a Jewish hatter. Perhaps his most magnificent performance was his own life; not until long after his death was his claim to noble birth, to a career as cavalry officer, and to the "von" which nobody ever disputed, proved to have been a myth of his own creation. He arrived in the States somewhere between 1906 and 1909, and drifted eventually to Hollywood. In 1914 he acted in *The Birth of a Nation* (it was his third film as an actor) and established himself as an assistant to Griffith. He fulfilled the same dual role on *Intolerance* (1916), and he worked as assistant to John Emerson, making his acting début in a leading role in *Old Heidelberg* (1915).

At the end of the war Stroheim managed to interest Carl Laemmle in a story which was made as *Blind Husbands* (1919). The triangle melodrama was not particularly significant; but the psychological observation, particularly in the treatment of the leading character of the callous, charming, elegant seducer, played by Stroheim himself, was entirely new, and pointed the direction of Stroheim's maturer work. It was the first of a trilogy on adultery; and was followed by *The Devil's Passkey* (in the phenomenal length of twelve reels; Stroheim always made films at a length which permitted detailed psychological exposition; and it was his undoing with producers). Based on a story by Baroness de Meyer, this now lost film must have been fascinating as an early picture of Americans in Europe, exposed to the perils of "continental" morality.

The most distinguished of the trio and the first great film of Stroheim's maturity, was *Foolish Wives* (1922). The essential plot (as frequently was the case with his films) was sheer novelette; what mattered was his analysis of character and of a strangely artificial society — the plot concerns international adventurers operating on the Côte d'Azur and the ruin they bring to their victims, whether rich American *émigrés* or wretched peasants. A brilliant, comic, brutal film, it is a richly detailed vision of the squalors and splendours of a particular area of post-war international society.

Foolish Wives was issued in a much mutilated version; and from that time no Stroheim film ever appeared in the form in which he had intended it. His next picture, and his last for Universal, was taken out of his hands by Thalberg and finished by Rupert Julian. *Merry-Go-Round* (1922) was the first in a new trilogy — this time based on the pre-war world, the last days of the Hapsburg empire, and continued in *The Merry Widow* and *The Wedding March*, with its sequel *The Honeymoon*. Again the aristocratic hero is shown indulging a callous infatuation both for a girl of his own class and for a humble, devoted creature, the daughter of a fairground puppet showman. It is a favourite Stroheim situation.

For Goldwyn Stroheim shot his most extraordinary picture, *Greed* (1923-24), based on Frank Norris's naturalist novel, *McTeague*, which Stroheim determined to transfer literally and in all its detail to the screen. He finished the film in twenty-four reels; whereupon the studio put it into various hands (including those of Rex Ingram) in order to reduce it to convenient commercial proportions. The fragmentary form that was finally issued, and which remains our only evidence of Stroheim's intentions, suffers inevitably from imbalance and irregular continuity. It remains nevertheless a staggering film by any standards one cares to apply. With unremitting cruelty and clarity it depicts the break-up of relationships (in particular the marriage of the dentist McTeague and Trina his wife) and the disintegration of character under the pressures of obsessive greed. *Greed* is still incomparable by reason of Stroheim's uncompromising realism, the performances of hitherto minor actors, Gibson Gowland, Jean Hersholt, Zasu Pitts, the use of actual locations, whether the poor streets of San Francisco or the sewer where the lovers woo, or Death Valley where the final terrifying confrontation of the male protagonists takes place.

Stroheim was next obliged to undertake what looked at first like a commercial chore — an adaptation of *The Merry Widow*, to star John Gilbert and Mae Murray. Nevertheless he succeeded in transforming it into something authentically Stroheimian, consigning the original plot to a mere epilogue, and offering a black comedy in a Ruritanian (or, rather, Hapsburgian) setting, rich in the cruelty and perversion and sadism which Stroheim perceived behind the decorous and romantic exteriors of the world of Lehar's operetta.

In his final great masterpiece, *The Wedding March* (the sequel, *The Honeymoon* was intended by Stroheim to make part of one complete film; but Paramount released it separately in a re-edition by Sternberg designed to make the second half complete in itself), the social setting is more precise. This actually is Vienna in the declining years of the Hapsburg dynasty. The class-erotic theme has a new slant in that the story tells of a marriage of convenience between the old aristocracy and the new aristocracy of industrial wealth. It is (or in the case of *The Honeymoon,* was — for the last surviving print seems now to have been destroyed) a film of thrilling plastic quality: the splendours of Imperial Vienna are a stage for human putrefaction, the whole somehow symbolised by the image of the bride, hobbling on her crippled foot up the aisle of the magnificent cathedral. The wedding night (which opened *The Honeymoon*) was a remarkable and horrifying scene: the groom's urbane expression of revulsion at his bride's physical deformity (he discovers it as he removes her shoes and stockings with fetishist gallantry) was unforgettable; it had a sophistication undreamed of by the so-called sophisticates of contemporary Hollywood.

Stroheim repudiated his last silent film, *Queen Kelly* (1928). In fact he had shot little more than third of it when it ran into trouble. The star, Gloria Swanson, walked off the set. The consequent delay in production meant that the film was outdated by the arrival of talking pictures, and the producer Joseph Kennedy abandoned the film. Those sections which were later assembled by Gloria Swanson, however, reveal Stroheim's hand and preoccupations, and the unique fantasy which found its favourite themes in madness, perversion and the mask-like face of a monarchical society in dissolution. It is sad that the collaboration of Stroheim and Swanson (who appeared together in *Sunset Boulevard* twenty-two years later) was never pursued. She was a perfect Stroheim heroine: few players could have carried off as she did the incredible first scene in which as a schoolgirl gazing at the prince as he gallops by on horseback, her knickers drop down, thereby unexpectedly catching the attention of the young man. No other director devised such an improbably unromantic first encounter for his hero and heroine.

After this Stroheim was destined never to release another film as director. The terror of producers who thought him impossibly extravagant, if not simply maniacal, he directed one more film, *Walking Down Broadway*, which was suppressed (and later completely re-made) as a result of internal studio warfare. Apart from this, Stroheim who had brought to the silent film a sophistication and maturity the cinema was hardly to know again, and a unique, disturbing and horrific vision of an old world in decay but still destructively lingering, was a houseless giant in the era of sound pictures. Intermittently he acted, in America and France, his performances as striking as his films had been. He left behind a heart-breaking trail of unrealised projects. Hollywood's failure to contain this trying genius is one of the tragedies of the history of art.

★ ★ ★

The other "von", **JOSEF VON STERNBERG**, had no more right to that distinction that von Stroheim; but he never pretended he had; it was given him by a producer who thought it looked more symmetrical on the titles. He too was born in Vienna. His family came to the States in 1901, returned, came back in 1908. The following year Josef found work in a millinery establishment. By 1914 he was employed as a film patcher with the World Film Company in New York. Then he became assistant to William A. Brady, World's director-general and the father of Alice Brady, with the responsibility of cutting and editing World Film Company's productions. In the war he served in the Army Signals Corps, whose cameramen at various times included Victor Fleming, George Hill, Ernest Schoedsack, Alan Crosland and Wesley Ruggles. For several years after the war Sternberg worked as assistant to a variety of directors in the United States and Great Britain — a subordinate position that must have been tiresome to a man of his legendary arrogance and ambition, had it not been for the hard-headed determination to acquire experience of the medium. By 1924 he had scripted Roy William Neill's *By Divine Right* and directed a couple of scenes left unfinished by another director.

Then he was approached by George K. Arthur, the English actor, to direct a film — made at a cost of under $5,000 and on distinctly shaky credit. Arthur was his leading man. A paid actor could only be afforded for one day's work, so for the rest of the time Sternberg made do with the character's shadow. But poverty meant independence, and Sternberg attempted something new: "Instead of the Elinor Glyn plots of the day, I had in mind a visual poem. Instead of flat lighting, shadows. In the place of pasty masks, faces in relief, plastic and deep-eyed. Instead of scenery which meant nothing, an emotionalised background that would transfer itself into my foreground. Instead of saccharine characters, sober figures moving in rhythm. Instead of stars I had engaged extras, and instead of extras I had planned to use a well-known star for one or two scenes. And dominating all this was an imposing piece of machinery: the hero of the film was to be a dredge." ("Fun in a Chinese Laundry", Secker and Warburg, 1966.) Today the interest of this film, *The Salvation Hunters* (1925), is largely historical.

The naturalist presentation of the world of waterfront derelicts was something new; and already in this film Sternberg's characteristic pre-occupations are signalled. His rich pictorialism, his way of lighting his pictures, his symbolism (the ever-present shadow of the dredge), added to the novelty of the circumstances in which the film was made, impressed Hollywood. United Artists took the film and Mary Pickford asked Sternberg to direct her next picture. Pickford was unenthusiastic about Sternberg's idea of a film called *Backwash*, which was to concern "a blind girl and a deaf mute, the subject to be visualised through the eyes of a girl who has never been able to see." So Sternberg passed to M-G-M. His first film there, *The Exquisite Sinner*, was re-made by Philip Rosen; his second, *The Masked Bride*, was given to Christy Cabanne after Sternberg, bored with his actors, began to photograph the studio roof instead. Next Chaplin asked him to make a film to provide a come-back for Edna Purviance. This legendary picture, *The Seagull* (1926), a psychological love story of great plastic beauty (reputedly) has never been shown. This series of catastrophes was understandably painful to Sternberg, who felt himself "a joke and the butt of every comment". For a while he was obliged to work as assistant director.

In 1926 however he impressed B. P. Schulberg of Paramount with his salvage work on Frank Lloyd's *Children of Divorce*, and was rewarded by being given *Underworld* to direct. The story was by Ben Hecht, who telegraphed Sternberg when the film was finished (in a flat four weeks), "You poor ham take my name off the film." Paramount did not like the film any better, until a dearth of product obliged them to sneak it into a Times Square cinema without publicity or press reviews. Its immediate and staggering success, which at once launched Sternberg's career anew, may well have been largely due to the subject; it was, practically speaking, the first gangster film. But even forty years afterwards it remains one of the best of the genre, and possibly Sternberg's most successful silent film. The story is taut and the sentimentality firmly controlled. It is about a tough gangster (George Bancroft) devoted to his girl friend Feathers (Evelyn Brent) and with a fascinated affection for his *protégé*, a cultivated but drunken little lawyer (Clive Brook). While the gangster is in prison, Feathers and Rolls Royce, the lawyer, find themselves falling in love. The gangster escapes; but understands the uprightness of their affection, and their undiminished loyalty to him, before he is shot by the police. In an exemplary way Sternberg uses his pictorial and lighting effects as a dynamic means to illuminate character and motivate the action. The melodrama — the first confrontation of Bull Weed and Rolls Royce, the jewel-store hold-up; the night-club shooting in which Bull kills a rival gangster; in particular Bull's own death — are done with an economy and accuracy that even Sternberg did not always equal.

The Last Command (1928) has not been seen for many years (again Paramount seem to have been unenthusiastic, though it proved ultimately a success with the public). The story is intriguing: a one-time

White Russian general is reduced to playing as an extra in films. Sternberg shows his two lives and the two personalities which they produce in the same man. Sternberg's view of the Hollywood scene at that time must have been pretty revealing; and everyone who saw the film agreed it was dramatic and polished. Sternberg's own account of the making of the film is mostly concerned with the difficulties he experienced with the capricious Emil Jannings. So unhappy was he working with the star, that he handed over another script he had written for him to be directed, as *Street of Sin*, by Mauritz Stiller.

In *The Drag Net* (1928), Sternberg returned to a gangster theme: the story is about a detective bent on running a gang of hijackers out of town, and who attracts the admiration and consequent assistance of the moll of one of the gangsters. Again, as in *Underworld*, Sternberg's pictorialism proved an entirely dynamic and in no way static element: the story and its characters are developed through well-observed visual detail. *The Docks of New York* (1928) is also set in the urban underworld in which Sternberg found scope for his taste for the picturesque. The simple story can give no idea of its masterly execution. George Bancroft saves a girl from suicide and marries her. He also saves her from a false charge of murder, and undergoes a prison sentence to clear her of a further charge of theft. The girl is understandably grateful. Sternberg's pleasure in the film evidently came from setting off the contrasting personalities of Olga Baclanova and Betty Compson.

For his last silent film, *The Case of Lena Smith* (1929), Sternberg returned to the world of his childhood, Vienna in the Nineties. The film was only released when talkies were well in vogue, and had little success in its own time. A strongly atmospheric piece, again with a fairly thin story about a peasant girl (Esther Ralston) wronged by a profligate young officer (James Hall) it is essentially an atmospheric piece, looking forward to the later sound films of Sternberg's great period. Like all of Sternberg's films from *Underworld* to *The Devil is a Woman*, *The Case of Lena Smith* was designed by Hans Dreier, who had come to Paramount in the early Twenties from U.F.A. (where he had designed Buchoweski's *Danton*) and E.F.A. and must have made a considerable contribution to Sternberg's films. But Sternberg is not overly inclined to acknowledge his collaborators (he manages to make no single mention of Dreier in his autobiography); and it must be admitted that though he worked with several cameramen of individual distinction, he still succeeded in imposing a unique visual style on his work, whether individual films were photographed by Bert Glennon, Harold Rosson, Lucien Ballard, Lee Garmes or Sternberg himself.

This is not the only enigma about Sternberg, whose pride and belligerence, which make him compulsively search for enemies, have not helped critical evaluation any more than they helped his Hollywood career. Inevitably the silent films have been overshadowed by his talkies; but a general reappraisal and a reconsideration of the old view of his films as being "static" and dedicated to purely pictorial effects is surely overdue.

* * *

Apart perhaps from Chaplin (and even he has suffered from a troubled private life and bitter periods of personal unpopularity) the happiest of all this group of artists is **JOHN FORD** (born, Sean Aloysius Feeley, in 1895). Ford has "never thought about what I was doing in terms of art, or 'this is great', or 'world-shaking', or anything like that. To me it was always a job of work — which I enjoyed immensely — and that's it." (Peter Bogdanovich: "John Ford", Studio Vista, 1968); and he has been able to pursue his vocation with no more than the predictable irritations and interferences from producers for more than half a century. At the time of writing Ford, at 73, has two projects currently in preparation.

Ford is a great story-teller both on and off the screen, and a degree of Celtic poeticism has inevitably crept into stories of his life. He seems to have been the youngest of eleven (or thirteen) children of an Irishman who came to the United States at fifteen to fight in the Civil War (the side, it seems, was immaterial) but arrived too late. Young Sean Feeley's aspirations as a youth are misty. He may have been designed for the priesthood, and he may have had ambitions to be an artist. He failed to get entrance to the Annapolis Naval College, and spent a brief three weeks at the University of Maine, before following his elder brother Francis to Hollywood. Francis, or Frank, Ford was then acting in serials for Universal. (Peter Bogdanovich's "John Ford" quotes Ford's very funny explanation of how Frank, and then he, adopted their professional surnames.) John, or Jack, worked as a prop boy, general assistant and occasional stand-in or stuntman for his brother.

All Ford's early work was on Westerns, and he was to become the greatest poet of the Western saga. In 1917 Laemmle set him to direct a series starring Harry Carey as Cheyenne Harry. He turned out two-reelers at a remarkable rate, generally without a script, improvising action around a rough scenario which the star and director would work out in a pleasantly informal fashion. Even as early as *Bucking Broadway* (1917), but especially after *The Outcasts of Poker Flat* (1919), reviewers praised the pictorial sense of the pictures. (Ford told Peter Bogdanovich, ". . . the only thing I always had was an eye for composition — I don't know where I got it — and that's all I did have".) Jean Mitry, who recalls these pictures, most of which have now disappeared, speaks of the development of a distinctive style even as early as this, "hacking away inessentials, in order to enclose the movement of the film in a violent, dynamic continuity, each image like a blow from a clenched fist . . ."

In 1920 Ford began to broaden his interests to take in such films as *The Prince From Avenue A*, a New York Irish comedy, starring Gentleman Jim Corbett, the boxer; but most of the fifty or so films (the precise count is lost) he made in his first seven years as a director were Westerns as broadly speaking was his first great film, *The Iron Horse* (1924). The film began as "quite a simple little story" but when Ford's unit went on location in Nevada, the project grew and grew until finally it became a vast epic of the building of the trans-continental railroad. A four-week schedule stretched into months. Blizzards where fair weather had been expected inspired new spectacle. Ford built miles of railroad track, and a shanty town; he re-created in fact as well as in his film the setting of a rough pioneer period. A much better film than *The*

Covered Wagon, it was an immense popular success on its release, earned over two million dollars for Fox and established Ford as a leading director.

It was however, some time before he repeated the artistic achievement of this film. Indeed his next seven features — *Hearts of Oak* (1924), *Lightnin'*, *Kentucky Pride* (1925), *The Fighting Heart* (1925), *Thank You* (1925), *The Shamrock Handicap* (1926) and *The Blue Eagle* (1926) — seem to have been fairly routine commercial products, only occasionally illuminated by Ford's grand grasp of character and his sense of the drama of natural locations. Indeed, Ford seemed for a time left behind by the self-conscious "sophistication" of films of the period. But *Three Bad Men* (1926), the story of three chivalrous outlaws in the pioneering Seventies, captured Ford's imagination, and practically equalled the achievement of *The Iron Horse*. Ford recalls that many of his players had actually taken part in land rushes, and remembered details, which were incorporated into the film. Again the breadth and humanity with which the characters are conceived, the unforced humour, the splendour of the setting (Jackson Hole) and of the action, lift the film into a class of its own.

Mother Machree (1927) was a lachrymose story of mother love, starring the inimitable Belle Bennett; but *Four Sons* (1928) was Ford's own choice of subject. The theme of a family divided by outside pressures was one which seems always to have attracted Ford. An enormous money-maker, its handling was the first sign of that consciously "aesthetic" quality which in equal degrees has tended to enrich and (in such a film as *The Informer*) to debilitate Ford's vision. Ford's last all-silent film was *Hangman's House* (1928), another Irish story. After a three-reel *conte*, *Napoleon's Barber*, and a couple of insignificant comedy dramas, *Riley the Cop* (1928) and *Strong Boy* (1929), both with synchronised music and sound effects, Ford made his first feature-length talkie, *The Black Watch* (1929), the talking scenes directed by Lumsden Hare, a Broadway dialogue "expert". Ford's great years as a director were still to come. His reputation as a silent director rested (and would still be secure if he had made nothing else) on two, or perhaps three, of the sixty films he had made in the course of twelve years.

* * *

Like Ford, **ROBERT J. FLAHERTY** was of Irish descent. As with Chaplin, the importance of his films lies more in their content than in any formal innovation. Like Stroheim he could never bring himself into accommodation with the world of commercial film-making, so that his output over the course of thirty years was very small. And like all the other film-makers considered in this chapter, his work expresses a coherent human personality, and remains faithful to his overriding preoccupations and sympathies. His films have been criticised for their ethnographical untruth and excessive "romanticism", but Flaherty's essential integrity, the steadiness of his own image of the world, his affection for the insignificant people of simple cultures — whether the esquimaux of the Arctic or the artisans of Thirties Britain — give his films a poetic validity.

Flaherty's upbringing now seems impossibly remote and romantic. He was born in Iron Mountain, Michigan, where his father ran an iron ore mine. When mining slumped his father prospected for gold, and at 12 Flaherty was living in a prospecting camp, getting his education from the lore of the Red Indians. He read and lived the novels of Fenimore Cooper and R. M. Ballantyne. In his teens he developed a passion and a talent for exploration, and made a number of expeditions around Hudson Bay, Ungava, Baffin Land and the mysterious Belcher Islands, one of which now bears the name of Flaherty Island. On one of these expeditions he took a moving picture camera as a recording instrument. Through carelessness all the material he shot on this trip was lost; but the results encouraged Flaherty to plan a film on the life of the esquimaux, and he obtained sponsorship for *Nanook of the North* from the Revillon Fur Company. Having edited his finished film he found considerable difficulty in selling it, but finally Pathe managed to get some distribution for it by double-billing it with *Grandma's Boy*. Nor was its critical reception entirely favourable. It became fashionable for Twenties intellectuals to impugn its anthropological authenticity. But, as Flaherty said, in a profound summing-up of the principles of all art, "Sometimes you have to lie. One often has to distort a thing to catch its true spirit." What mattered in *Nanook* was not the ethnographical placing of a primitive society so much as Flaherty's ability to convey the way of life of a primitive man entirely without patronage, without sensationalism, and yet so as to discover in the daily life of this rather jolly person and his simple family the very essence, the quintessence of the human struggle for existence. In that the struggle was a material one, while America in a time of prosperity was more concerned with psychological and ethical dilemmas, the film was escapist, romantic; and this in itself alienated the sympathy of the realists who represented the vanguard of intellectualism.

Jesse Lasky, personally enthusiastic about exploration, and eager for prestige movies, financed Flaherty on a trip to the South Seas to try to repeat the success of *Nanook*. Frederick O'Brien, the author of *White Shadows in the South Seas*, told him that Sawaii was the last remaining island uncorrupted by Western civilisation. In fact Flaherty found it a maladministered, corrupt place, unofficially ruled over by a crazed old German queen. He found the islanders given to feuding; his lab-boys were involved in a murder; and when the Flahertys tried to defend them they were themselves accused of trying to pervert the course of justice. Added to that, Flaherty himself was seriously ill during part of the many months that he spent on the island.

Undaunted, Flaherty created in *Moana* a poetic fantasy of the uncorrupted, traditional life of the islanders. He re-created or created ancient and vanished traditions. He paid his principal actor highly to undergo the painful tattooing ceremony which was altogether obsolete and which in the normal course of things the boy would not have dreamed of suffering. Divorced from reality, the film remains a hypnotically lovely dream of paradise — ethnographically unfounded, but with a conviction of its own. The plastic qualities of the film — shot in panchromatic stock which gives the black-and-white images a unique texture — are exceptional. Despite Paramount's attempt to sell the film as "The Love Life of a South Sea Siren", *Moana* did disappointing business, and damaged Flaherty's reputation in Hollywood. He made two privately sponsored shorts (*The Pottery Maker*, financed by Maude Adams, and *24 Dollar Island*) neither of which seems to have been very good, and talked about a colour version of *Kim* — a project which foreshadowed the later *Elephant Boy*.

Next, Flaherty was invited by M-G-M to direct *White Shadows of the South Seas* in collaboration with Willard S. Van Dyke; but his colleague's approach to the subject was utterly repugnant to him, as was working with big stars; and he returned to Hollywood. In 1928 he began a picture about the Pueblo Indians for Fox; but later in the year he met F. W. Murnau, and abandoned the film, which was going badly because of disagreements with Fox, to go to the South Seas with the German director. The outcome of that unfortunate project has already been described in Chapter 4. Flaherty subsequently came to Europe where two of the three features and one of the two shorts which comprised the whole output of the remaining twenty years of his activity, were made.

Hollywood was not an easy place for the individualist, the nonconformist and the genius.

8. The Idols

THE TWENTIES was the age of idols: aeronauts, baseball players, preachers, politicians, but above all — movie stars. It was not just by chance that the greatest of all the gods in the Hollywood pantheon all belonged, pre-eminently, to the post-war decade — Pickford, Fairbanks, Chaplin, Valentino, Garbo. The silent stars had a magic that could never quite be recaptured in days of talking pictures. The lack of voices did not constitute a deficiency in a specific human attribute. On the contrary, distancing them from ordinary human normality, it added to the mystery and romance and remoteness of the image. "It's the pictures that got small," said Norma Desmond; and she was right, in that sound brought the stars a significant degree nearer to reality. Since talking pictures it has been impossible to imagine the wild, nation-wide enthusiasm that greeted Chaplin or Pickford/Fairbanks on their various European trips, or the manifestos at Valentino's funeral. Beatlemania at its height is in no sense comparable.

And inevitably it was in the Twenties that the star system as we know it today was evolved. Stars like Pickford and Mabel Normand were created by the public without any significant intervention of studio machinery intended for the fabrication of stars. Indeed, as late as 1910, producers zealously kept their artists from becoming stars, and went to considerable lengths to keep their personal identities secret so as to restrain them from demanding salaries in relation to their individual drawing power. The first star to be known by her own name to the public was Florence Lawrence, the Biograph Girl, and then it was only because Carl Laemmle, having won her from Biograph for his own I.M.P. Studio, organised a huge newspaper stunt to publicise his new acquisition.

By 1918, of course, those happy days of innocent anonymity were long past. In 1915 Fox had shown the way to modern star promotion methods in selling Theda Bara to the public. By the end of the war Mary Pickford was earning 350,000 dollars a picture, with bonuses, and Chaplin had signed to make eight two-reelers for Mutual for a clear million dollars, with bonuses. The bankers and accountants and men from the rag trade could not ignore commodities of such value. Within a decade the star system was organised on industrial principles. "Producers found the trick," wrote Louise Brooks, "of curbing the stars and standardising their product according to their will and personal taste." But "it was never their will, but the public's which made them exploiters of great personalities and builders of enduring stars. It was never their taste, but that of certain writers and directors by which their product sometimes lost its passing value as entertainment and gained the enduring value of art." (*Sight and Sound*, Winter, 1958.)

'aude George and 'ich von Stroheim THE 'EDDING MARCH 927), a story set 'ainst the lendours of nperial Vienna and ven a thrilling astic quality by von 'roheim's direction.

Betty Compson and George Bancroft in Josef von Sternberg's THE DOCKS OF NEW YORK (1928), a simple story masterfully executed.

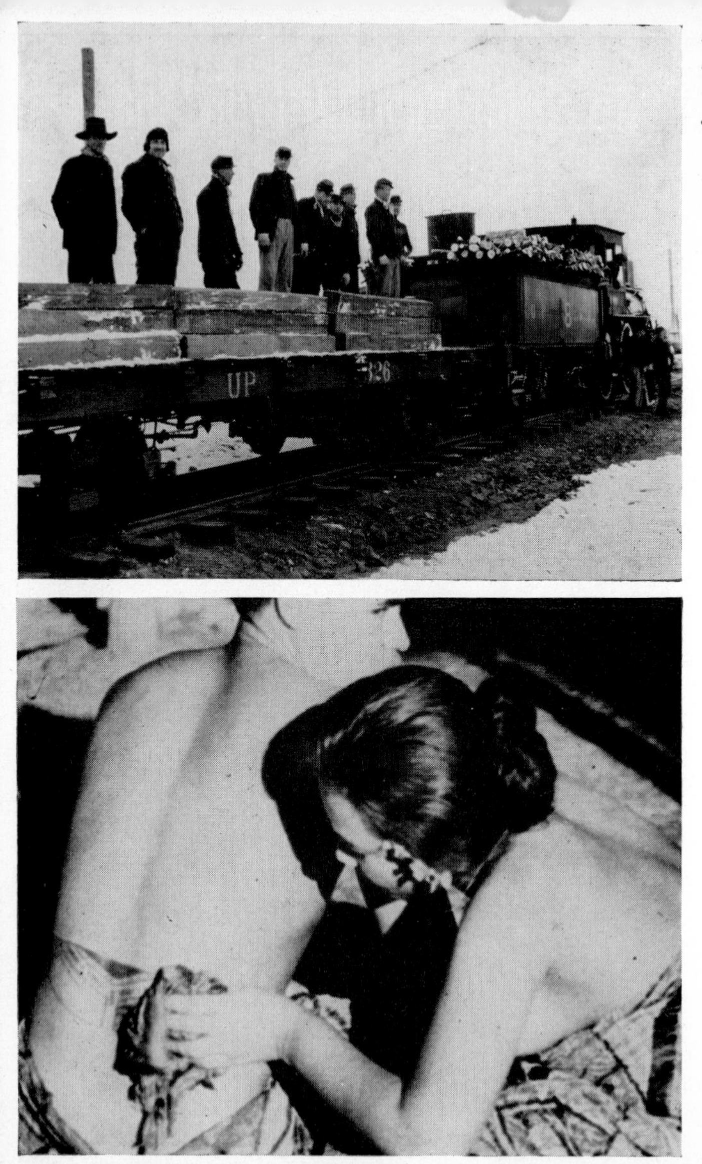

An epic of railroad construction: John Ford's THE IRON HORSE (1924).

"America Sweetheart Mary Pickfor with Charl Rogers in Sa Taylor's M BEST GIR (1927

Dougl Fairbanks, t idol of eve American bo with Lupe Vel in F. Richa Jones' TH GAUCHO (1927

The painful tattooing ceremony in Robert J. Flaherty's MOANA, filmed in the South Seas.

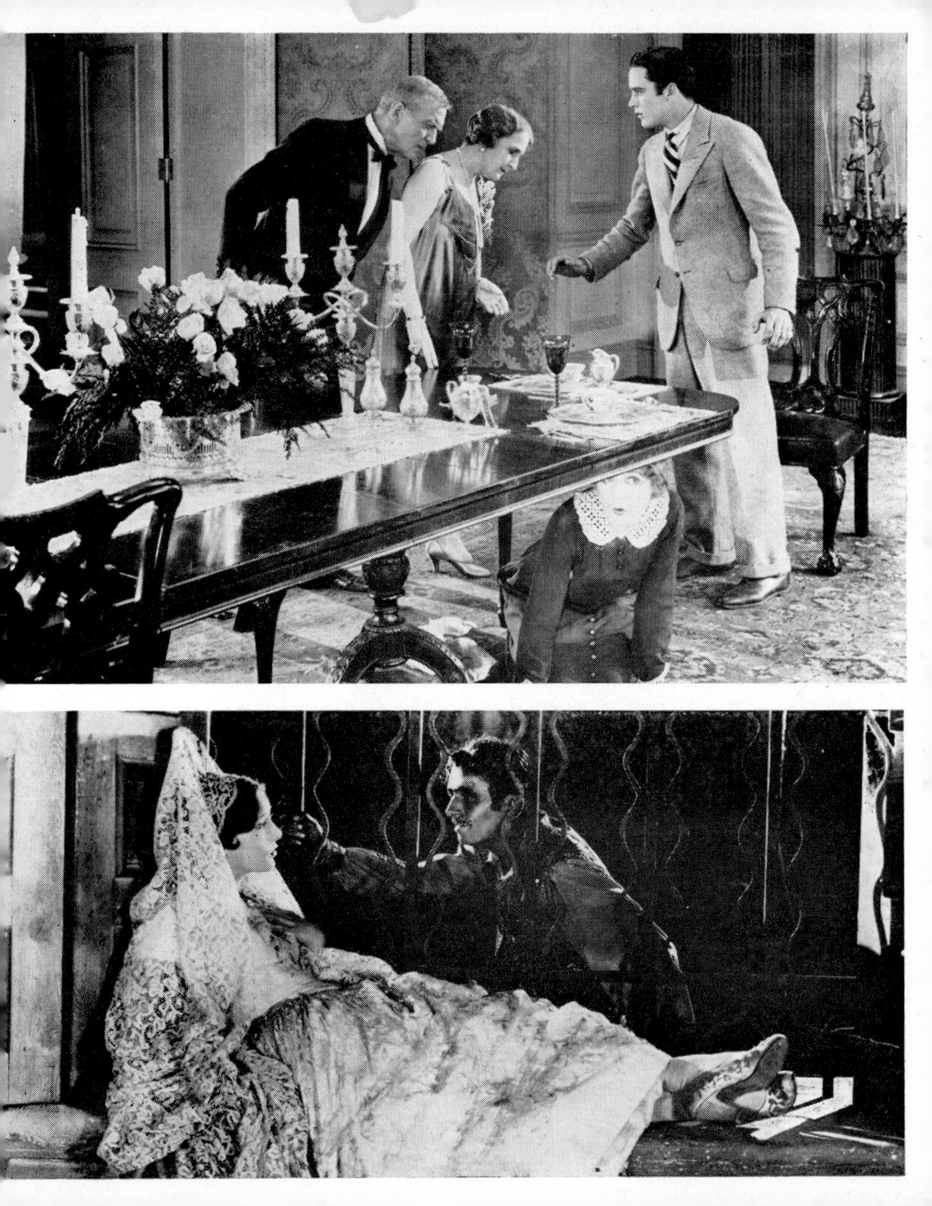

"It feels so good—just to be alive": Joan Crawford and friends in Harry Beaumont's OUR DANCING DAUGHTERS (1928).

A positive, aggressive sexuality Clara Bow with Percy Marmont in Victor Fleming's MANTRAP (1926) one of the films based on the work the literary nonconformist Sinclair Lewis.

★ ★ ★

The parade of screen idols of the Twenties reflects the changing tastes and the varied needs of America in those years. They were the heroes, ideals, fantasy projections of real and daily life. Some of them promised adventure and new kinds of exotic social or sexual experience. Others set out to reveal and reflect the more solid rewards of the homely and familiar. Some personified the new post-war morality, while others in their turn glorified traditional and rooted values. Some offered dreams; others consolation.

At the war's end the screen was still dominated by stars who represented solidly all-American values, the secure virtues of pre-war morality. Griffith of course had first put on the screen Mary Pickford, the Gishes, Mae Marsh, Blanche Sweet, Bessie Love; and something of the Victorian romanticism of Griffith's own outlook clung to these girls through much of their career.

MARY PICKFORD remains unique; a phenomenon as singular and important as was Garbo, a decade after her. Paul Rotha, never careless with compliments, wrote in 1930: "Both Mr. and Mrs. Douglas Fairbanks are extremely serious about this film business. They realise their responsibility. They are both of extreme importance to the cinema. With Chaplin, Stroheim, and, to a lesser extent, Griffith, they are the outstanding figures in the American cinema. It would be wise not to underestimate the value of their work. They have separately and jointly given much that is good to the film." The best assessment of Pickford's unquestionable talents and the extent to which she became a prisoner of her own legends — the legend of Little Mary, The Child with the Golden Curls, America's Sweetheart — is Alexander Walker's sympathetic essay in "The Celluloid Sacrifice" (Joseph, 1966).

She was born in Canada in 1893. Her father died when she was five and as a child actress on the stage she became the principal breadwinner for her mother and two younger children. In 1907 she joined Belasco, who changed her name from Gladys Smith and brought her to Broadway. In 1909 she shamefacedly took work at Biograph. Griffith, who at first thought her too fat, found in her an ideal Cinderella figure: her own lost childhood, her premature responsibilities gave a special poignancy to her portrayals in *The New York Hat* (1912) or (among many other early roles) *Tess of the Storm Country* (1914), *Cinderella* (1914), *Rags* (1915), *A Poor Little Rich Girl* (1917), *Rebecca of Sunnybrook Farm* (1917). This is not to suggest that she was not also a conscious actress of fine instincts and highly developed intelligence and skill.

An astute business woman, she moved from company to company in pursuit of higher salaries and greater independence. Her first post-war release, *Daddy Long Legs*, was distributed by First National. After this all her films were released through United Artists, of which, with Chaplin, Fairbanks and Griffith, she was a co-founder. Time and again she tried to break out of her image of a little girl; but always without success. The public forced her back to *Pollyanna* (1919), *Little Lord Fauntleroy* (1921), *Little Annie Rooney* (1925), *Sparrows* (1926), rejecting her in maturer roles as *Rosita* (1923) or *Dorothy Vernon of Haddon Hall* (1924). By the time that talking pictures came she was threatened with the fate of becoming a monstrous phenomenon — a woman in her middle thirties still playing child roles, a heroine of Victorian pathos lingering on into the jazz age. After four sound pictures which revealed a talent still capable of development, but which failed to make her public accept her in sophisticated adult roles, Miss Pickford retired, securely enshrined as one of the greatest Hollywood legends.

The Gish girls have never retired, though after the arrival of talking pictures they returned to the stage, where their careers had begun. They were brought to Griffith in 1912, by Mary Pickford who had acted with them in theatres soon after the turn of the century. **LILLIAN GISH** was a heroine straight out of the romantic poets Griffith knew and loved so well. Her extraordinary fragility, her spiritual vibrance, her unique, strange beauty often uplifted the more commonplace concepts of Griffith's Victorian sentiment. It is impossible to imagine *Broken Blossoms* or *Way Down East* without Gish: they would certainly not have survived as they have without her marvellous performances.

It is an interesting indication of Gish's creative approach to her acting to learn that she herself devised the form of the closet scene in the former film: "You know the scene in the closet, where I spin round and round in terror as Donald Crisp is trying to open the door to beat me and kill me. I worked that out myself, and never told Griffith what I was going to do. You see, if I had told him, he'd have made me rehearse it over and over again; and that would have spoilt it. It had to be spontaneous, the hysterical terror of a child. Well, when I came to play the scene in front of the camera, I did it as I'd planned — spinning and screaming terribly (I was a good screamer; Mr. Griffith used to encourage me to scream at the top of my voice). When we finished, Mr. Griffith was very pale. There was a man from *Variety* at the studio, and Mr. Griffith called him in and made me go through the scene again for him. It was so horrific that the man from *Variety* went outside and brought up his breakfast . . ." (interview with the author, published in *Sight and Sound*).

There are innumerable similar anecdotes of the extraordinary intensity of Gish's playing before the camera: how the baptism of the dying child in *Way Down East* was so real and affecting that the child's real, off-screen father fainted; how Vidor and everyone else on the set of *La Bohème* thought she really had died when they shot the death scene. Gish is by any standards a very great actress. Seeing such a performance as hers in *The Wind*, it is interesting, but bitter, to speculate what wonders she might have achieved if her career had carried on without interruption into the era of sound. But a new star eclipsed her at M-G-M which in 1925 had given her an $800,000 contract. After Garbo came, the studio put Miss Gish into routine chores, and then happily let her go before her contract was fulfilled. "Stigmatised as a grasping, silly, sexless antique, at the age of 31, the great Lillian Gish left Hollywood for ever, without a head turned to mark her departure," wrote Louise Brooks, not quite accurately, for in recent years Miss Gish has occasionally appeared in character roles in films, with notable distinction.

A lesser actress than Lillian Gish, **Mae Marsh**, was more limited by her initial typing as a Griffith sentimental heroine; and her popularity faded with unfortunate casting in the Twenties. Gamely she continued to work almost to the end of her life in character roles. Two other Griffith girls who on the contrary triumphed over type-casting were Blanche Sweet and Bessie Love. **Blanche Sweet** (born 1896) had joined Griffith at the same time as Pickford and was his star in *Judith of Bethulia*. After the war her career was threatened by an increasingly uncomfortable personality. Overwork, perhaps, had made her (in Harry Carr's words) "an exceedingly difficult and disagreeable girl." After two years away from the screen and her marriage to Marshall Neilan she seemed happier, and made a successful comeback. Her most distinguished performance in this period of her career was as Anna Christie in John Griffith Wray's first film version of the play, directed for Ince.

BESSIE LOVE was and remains one of the most endearing screen stars. Soon after her first appearance with Griffith in *Intolerance* a critic described her as "the sweetest, demurest, tenderest, most plaintive little thing on the screen" — which she was; but she is also an actress of pure instincts and impregnable sincerity. After her period as a sweet and demure Griffith heroine (with a roguish humour that was never quite submerged and which, in Triangle days, enabled her to hold her own as co-star to the ebullient young Fairbanks) she was able to move on to a career as a dramatic actress, though in the middle Twenties she was rarely given work worthy of her talents or which exploited the individual charm she radiated. Her real return to star status came with talking pictures when her vitality, her total lack of pretension and her sheer technique made her one of the first successful stars of film musicals.

However dated some of the master's sentiments, Griffith gave the actors and actresses who worked for him at Biograph and later at Triangle incomparable training which may explain the dominance of the Griffith type in the immediate post-war period. But Americans had other images of themselves besides frail, romantic Victorian beauties. There were tomboys and madcaps too. One of the most tragic figures of the silent era was **MABEL NORMAND.** A beautiful, irrepressibly vital girl and a brilliant clown and mimic, her special gift was her complete naturalness in front of the camera. A scene like that in *Tillie's Punctured Romance*, in which she reacts to the unsought attentions of a fat and aged lecher beside her in a cinema, is not only funny but exactly true. She began her career as an artist's model, became an extra at Biograph and was finally realised by the direction of Mack Sennett. Their amorous bickering constantly interrupted Mabel's career. After numerous shorts, some with Arbuckle and Chaplin, Sennett put her into a feature, *Mickey* (1918), whose subtle comedy is perhaps better appreciated today than in its own time. Restlessness, induced perhaps by ill health in turn aggravated (according to Anita Loos) by narcotics, led her to leave Sennett for Goldwyn, only to return after fifteen pictures, none of them particularly successful. Sennett produced the now ailing Normand in four more films, *Molly O* (1921), *Oh Mabel Behave* (1922), *Suzanna* (1923), and *The Extra Girl* (1923). Meanwhile her popularity had been hard hit, by her being the last person to see the director William Desmond Taylor alive before his murder. Her marriage with Lew Cody caused an unredeemable rift between Sennett and Normand, and except for an unsuccessful attempt at a comeback with Hal Roach, she retired from the screen. Mabel Normand was one of the first stars to thrill her fans as much by her off-screen activity as by her performances. Her much publicised pranks — whether at home or on her European trips — and her fabulous wardrobe established a style which has been often imitated by her successors.

PEARL WHITE, the girl who battled her way through episode after episode of countless serials between 1914 and 1922, also lived a private life of no less colour — if of somewhat different style — than her screen appearances. On the screen — fighting rustlers, gamblers, gangsters, bandits, smugglers with fine impartiality — she provided war-time and post-war America with an athletic and recognisably native heroine.

★ ★ ★

When, in 1920, Mary Pickford was married to **DOUGLAS FAIRBANKS**, it was the culmination of an American dream. While Pickford was America's Sweetheart, Fairbanks was the idol of every American boy. Unlike most of his Hollywood acting contemporaries, Fairbanks was born into a comfortable middle-class background: his father was a lawyer. His early years were characteristically restless: acting a bit, studying law, three mysterious months at Harvard, a hardware store, drifting in Europe, acting a bit more. By the start of 1915 he had evidently become a notable enough actor for Harry Aitken to sign him with Triangle; but neither Griffith nor the Triangle personnel appreciated his tiresome high spirits and energy.

It appears to have been the young scenarist Anita Loos and the director John Emerson who first perceived the possibilities in Fairbanks's relentless high spirits and athletic presence; and began the series of scenarios which established him as the American archetype of normality and go and pep. Today the go and pep — at least in the early films — seem as irritating as the same qualities in the real-life Doug appeared to his first collaborators at Triangle. When, for instance, in *Manhattan Madness* he returns from the West to his New York club and starts to floor all the Eastern weaklings with his back slapping, he looks nowadays a ludicrous caricature of the extrovert personality. But to his own generation he was the ideal of the healthy man, the priest of the Roosevelt strenuous life, fighting the enfeebling encroachments of over-civilisation. With a virility and an enthusiasm and an optimism that caught the imagination of the times, Fairbanks made more than two dozen films that combined cheerful fast adventure with good-natured satires on American fads, foibles and manners. "He laughed at hypochondriacs, in Dr. Jollyem's Long Island sanitarium for rich neurotics (*Down to Earth*); at "bean-can nobility" in the person of Leander Hick, manufacturer of the One Hump Hat-Pin (*American Aristocracy*); Anglophilia (*Mr. Fix-It* and *The Mollycoddle*); success literature (*Reaching for the Moon*); bachelor girls, bobbed hair and patronising social work (*The Nut*); the Eastern clubman (*Knickerbocker Buckaroo*); quack psychologists (*When the Clouds Roll By*);

and by the way, in casual dissolves and pointed subtitles expressed himself unambiguously on the subject of modern dancing, Couéism, ouija boards, night club entertainment, women's clothes and other incidental oddities of the period" (Alistair Cooke in "Douglas Fairbanks: The Making of a Screen Character"; Museum of Modern Art N.Y., 1940). Fairbanks's creative contribution to the films — quite apart from his performances — is unquestionable. Increasingly he supervised every aspect of their making; he wrote quite a number of his own stories; and certainly contributed much to their direction. Testimony to the rapidity with which Fairbanks had established himself as a symbol of young America and American Go is that in 1917, barely two years after his first entry into pictures, a peak in the Yosemite National Park was named after him. The titles of Fairbanks's immediate post-war films — *He Comes Up Smiling*, *The Knickerbocker Buckaroo*, *His Majesty the American*, *When The Clouds Roll By* — are significant of his particular role and his typical optimism.

In 1920 Fairbanks made *The Mollycoddle*, the last of his long series of skits on contemporary manners. This was a very jolly comedy about a young man brought up in the enervating atmosphere of the French Riviera, who returns to his native West to find that exposure to the raw rough land brings out his latent inherited virility and enables him singlehanded to rout Wallace Beery and his gang of diamond smugglers.

After this Fairbanks embarked upon his series of elaborate costume spectacles — *The Mark of Zorro* (1920), *The Three Musketeers* (1921), *Robin Hood* (1922), *The Thief of Bagdad* (1923-4), *Don Q, Son of Zorro* (1925), *The Black Pirate* (1926), *The Gaucho* (1927), *The Iron Mask* (1929). But his fans were not fooled. It was still Doug, still the All-American optimist making his way, fulfilling everybody's dream of escape and triumph.

A significant element in Fairbanks's art as well as a factor in his immense appeal, was his phenomenal athleticism. He could do miracles: leap and vault and run with entirely abnormal skill. His feats enhanced his adventure; they *described* his high spirits, as a dancer's means express his feelings; and they enforced upon every one of Fairbanks's later films a rare grace and fluidity and rhythm. Fairbanks, as well as a symbol and a god, was one of the cinema's great intuitive artists in the years of silent movies.

Other heroes enshrined ideals of American life different from Fairbanks's combination of "the Roosevelt concept of the 'strenuous life' and the American worship of speed" (Lewis Jacobs). **Charles Ray** personified the simple virtues of rural America. Recruited to the cinema from the theatre by Ince, Ray did his best work under Ince's production. His attempts to establish his own production company and his work after Ince's death were never very successful, and by the middle Twenties his star had set. But for a time he delighted the nation with films like *The Hired Man* (1928), *An Old-Fashioned Boy* (1920) and *The Old Swimmin' Hole* (1921). But Ray's was a delicate talent, which has so far defied successful revival. **Richard Barthelmess** was a much more varied actor than Ray, as his roles with Griffith show (in *Broken Blossoms*, *Way Down East* and *The Idol Dancer* he played strongly contrasted characters); but after his enormous success in King's *Tol'able David* (1921) he, too, tended to be typed as the rural-rooted American boy.*

This was, of course, the great era of the Western star, though the nature of the Western was changing; and there is a sensible increase in sophistication between the rugged simplicity of **WILLIAM S. HART**'s Western heroes and (say) Gary Cooper, whose first Western roles came at the end of this period (he had arrived in Hollywood in 1926). Hart remains the greatest Western star. His noble, angular face at once marks him out as what he was — a nineteenth-century stage actor. He had played with Modjeska and Belasco, and already acted Western roles on the stage in the Nineties. In 1905 and 1907 respectively he created two of the most famous characters in the Western mythology: *The Squaw Man* and *The Virginian.*

Hart came to films in 1914 and continued in the cinema until 1925 when he made his excellent, last picture, King Baggott's *Tumbleweeds.* He is a strange figure now, with his stiff walk, his mirthless face, his

*The exceptions include his roles in *Shore Leave* and *Patent Leather Kid.*

mid-Victorian morality. (In Lambert Hillyer's *The Toll Gate*, adapted like many of Hart's films from his own novel, he removes his waistcoat in a lady's bedroom, and is so remorseful at this expression of unbridled passion that he hands himself over to the law.) And yet there is still an oddly noble, even poetic quality about the man — perhaps because of his very strangeness, perhaps because of the sentimental romanticism with which he invests the land and the horses and the heroines with whom he comes into contact; perhaps more because of the character which was to become a commonplace, but which he first created: the "good-bad man", the hero with a past for whom his present nobility is a kind of atonement, and who will always ride off into the sunset rather than commit another person to the burden of a lasting attachment.

Hart, despite his oddity, has a stature that none of the others, for all their varied fascinations, ever achieved — not even smiling, volatile **Tom Mix,** who could bring the West right up to date, as in Lynn Reynolds's *Sky High* (1922), where he is a government officer, using cars and — with splendid aerial material — aeroplanes to trap immigration smugglers. They had all their distinctive character and appeal: the humorous and rugged Harry Carey who was John Ford's favourite hero; the burly, extrovert Tim McCoy; Ken Maynard, handsome and urbane; the boyish, clown-faced Hoot Gibson; the gentle giant William Russell. The majority of the cowboy stars, like Mix, Gibson, Carey and Maynard, graduated from Wild West shows. Among the exceptions was **George O'Brien**, whose good looks and sensitive playing were unique. Although he was selected by Murnau for the leading role in *Sunrise*, O'Brien's most enduring roles are in the Westerns he made with Ford, *The Iron Horse* and *Three Bad Men.*

Jack Warren Kerrigan belonged to the era of Hart, but possessed an urbanity that seemed to belong rather to the end of the silent period. His sleek-haired quality enabled him to move easily from Western hero roles to social comedies; but it eventually ended his career. After a brief absence from the screen he returned in 1923 to star in *The Covered Wagon*; but his formal good looks seemed at odds with the documentary qualities of the picture. His personal reception was disappointing, and after five more films he retired in 1924.

New film fashions in the early Twenties brought forward new styles of stars. The Pollyannas and Cinderellas of the pre-war cinema and the Biograph studios had no place in the sophisticated comedies of DeMille and Lubitsch and their followers, whose characters were men and women of the world. Among the male stars of this era, **ADOLPHE MENJOU** had no peer. Trained as an engineer, Menjou had drifted almost accidentally into acting, and though his poise and air of civilised amusement are already notable in *The Three Musketeers*, his real triumph was *A Woman of Paris*. After that Menjou was firmly typed through an endless series of sophisticated social comedies — *Broadway after Dark* (1924), *The Marriage Circle* (1924), *The Grand Duchess and the Waiter* (1926), *Are Parents People* (1926), and thirty or forty more of the same character. Menjou's genuine talent carried his career through the sound period and his own middle and old age.

An older artist whose distinguished stage background suited him to roles like the dancing father in *Dancing Mothers*, was **Conway Tearle.** A more bizarre Hollywood accession was Bernhardt's former leading man **Lou Tellegen** who, after a spasmodic career in Hollywood, found his forte in European charmer roles in films like *Single Wives* (1924), *The Breath of Scandal* (1925), *Parisian Nights* (1925) and *Married Alive* (1927). A native sophisticate, **Wallace Reid** was DeMille's star in *The Affairs of Anatol* (1921). Reid was the ideal all-American hero, handsome, suave, sophisticated, educated at Newark Military Academy. His early death from the results of alcohol and narcotics shattered an American dream of the Twenties.

In general Hollywood's women of the world outnumbered the men. **Clara Kimball Young** (1890-1960) had already specialised before the war in mature and sophisticated roles, and her career took a decided lift from the new fashions of the times. At the beginning of the post-war period she was still a valuable enough property to have a million-dollar company built around her; but her star set rather quickly after she abandoned Myron Selznick's astute management to make her new husband her impresario. The results were disastrous enough for Miss Young to leave films for vaudeville between 1924-5 and 1931, when she attempted a modest comeback. **Anna Q. Nilsson,** the beautiful Swedish actress, could turn with equal facility from the role of W. S. Hart's leading lady in *The Toll Gate* to elegant heroines or to a piquant blonde style in vamps. **Alice Terry** was recruited to Triangle in 1916 and proved an ideal heroine for Rex Ingram's romantic dramas. After *Four Horsemen of the Apocalypse* Ingram (whom she subsequently married) recognised the particular fascination in the opposition of Terry's cool and reserved beauty and the ardour of Latin lovers. He cast her with Novarro in *The Arab* (1924), with Moreno in *Mare Nostrum* (1926) and Petrovich in *The Garden of Allah* (1927) and *The Three Passions* (1929). **Florence Vidor,** the attractive wife of King Vidor, became a brilliant comedienne under the direction of Lubitsch and Mal St. Clair, though other aspects of her original talent were revealed in *Alice Adams* (1923) and *Main Street* (1923), in which she provided the perfect embodiment of Carol Kennicott. Both **Norma Talmadge** and **Norma Shearer** were actresses of style and talent whose careers were helped by fortunate marriages. The Talmadge sisters united in one family three of the most popular heroine types of the era. While Norma was essentially the elegant and sophisticated woman of the world, Constance was the ideal flapper. Natalie was only unwillingly and occasionally an actress; but in her husband's film *Our Hospitality* (1924), she proves a tractable sentimental heroine. The management of all three Talmadge girls was undoubtedly helped by the guidance of Norma Talmadge's husband Joseph Schenck.

Parenthetically it is worth noting the influence of Hollywood mothers. Margaret (Peg) Talmadge was evidently a formidable figure around the studios. Mrs. Gish was so horrified when she saw the things that were done to her little girls that she only set foot in the studios once; but this frail, ailing woman had nevertheless a great influence over her wonderful daughters. (A refreshingly realistic one, too. When the girls ran home one day to report with excitement that they had been recognised in the street and that people had turned to stare, she chilled their enthusiasm by pointing out that people would stare equally if they wore rings through their noses.) Mrs. Pickford, Mrs. Sennett and Mrs. Loos were also respected and fearfully loved in Hollywood, the confidantes of all their children's friends and co-workers.

The most enchanting stars invented by the Twenties were the flapper girls, seen at their inspired best in the young Joan Crawford, Gloria Swanson, Colleen Moore, Clara Bow, Louise Brooks, Sally O'Neil and Marion Davies. As befitted the times, they were different in quality from the clowning of Mabel Normand. They are tough and pretty and saucy, with endless funds of resource and energy and wit and spirit. They dance till dawn, then Charleston all the way home. They admire good-looking men without embarrassment or inhibition, and pursue them without reserve. But generally speaking their toughness is exercised to protect their purity, not to dispose of it; and the man who gets "fresh" (which may mean no more than a peck in the back of a cab) may end up with a sock on the jaw. Or if he is too much of a gentleman for that sort of treatment, the girl will get out of the car and walk home. "It feels so good — just to be alive," exclaims Wild Diana Merrick (Joan Crawford) in *Our Dancing Daughters*; and the joy, the celebration of youth and beauty and success, the zest of these girls and of the age itself communicates itself as vividly (and as poignantly) as anything in the silent cinema.

GLORIA SWANSON remains the most distinguished of the whole group. A graduate from the Sennett Bathing Beauties (a classic stepping stone to success, as King Vidor's enchanting *Show People* records), via Fox Sunshine Comedies and an interesting but little known series of dramas made for Triangle, her sophisticated wit and verve was recognised by DeMille, for whom she made a run of six comedies which established her as a symbol of American female *chic*. Her spirit and versatility prevented her from ever being typed. She could alternate the flapper with the woman of the world, Madame Sans Gêne and the fool kitchen help in *Stage Struck* who ends up on amateur night in a vaudeville show, with a sock pulled down over her face and boxing with a female giant. (Later in the same film she falls over the side of a show-boat but is caught on a handy hook by the seat of her pants. "Oh Lord," prays the Captain, "Give strength to her trousers.") In 1928 Swanson played her greatest dramatic roles, in *Sadie Thompson* and Stroheim's *Queen Kelly*, which she herself produced and completed.

Like Swanson, **Marion Davies**, who began her professional career as a dancer and subsequently a Ziegfeld girl was a spirited comedienne, though the spirit was somewhat curbed by W. R. Hearst, who forbade, for instance, the shying of custard pies at her in Vidor's *Show People*. **Colleen Moore**, with her bob, was a gentler actress than these two, easier with sentimental roles like *Irene* (1926) or *Lilac Time*, although renowned as the original screen flapper. Despite a period in two-reel comedy, Miss Moore's career was very much coloured by her beginnings under Griffith; and her chance to reveal herself in a dramatic role came in *So Big* (1925). Among stars of the second rank, **Sally O'Neil**, first discovered by Marshall Neilan, is memorable for her charming performance in Keaton's *Battling Butler* and Edmund Goulding's *Sally, Irene and Mary*, in which her co-stars were **Constance Bennett** and **Joan Crawford**. Crawford at this period had an irresistible vivacity, and already much of that compelling quality of personality that transcended questions of mere talent to make her a great star of three succeeding decades. Constance Bennett was generally easier in roles more sophisticated than the flapper type.

LOUISE BROOKS was in a special class. Her German films revealed her as an actress of great interior power; but she was condemned in her Hollywood years (1926-7) to undistinguished flapper roles (*Love 'Em and Leave 'Em*, *The Showoff*, *Just Another Blonde*, *Rolled Stockings* et al.). Only in later films — Howard Hawks's *A Girl in Every Port* (1929) and *The Canary Murder Case* (1929)—did she achieve the sort of artistic distinction she had demonstrated in her films for Pabst.

CLARA BOW managed, wrote Anita Loos, with terse ungenerosity, "At the same time to be innocuous and trashy." Her childhood was very poor, but at the age of seventeen a beauty contest took her to Hollywood. Bow characteristically "kept to roles within the average American girl's experience (and pay packet). She was a manicurist, usherette, waitress, cigarette girl, taxi driver, swimming instructress and salesgirl generally found around the lingerie department. All were roles in the range of promiscuous but legal employment where a girl can flirt with an ever changing male clientele. In these films Clara is lifted out of a milieu familiar to her flapper fans and shown the shopgirl's dream world of high life and wild parties" (Alexander Walker in "The Celluloid Sacrifice", Michael Joseph, 1966). She was insolent, beautiful and distinctly talented. Her lasting legend was established when Elinor Glyn, a fellow redhead, selected her to star in *It* (1927). She possessed a positive, aggressive sexuality: ". . . her highly individual way of projecting sexiness was by touch: she was always touching her man lightly and fleetingly, seldom lingering, as if she found it stimulating to break contact and come again." (*ibid.*)

★ ★ ★

RUDOLPH VALENTINO brought something entirely new to the cinema. Although he fulfilled a fantasy already long established in popular female literature, he topped it with new fantasies and new dreams. To the emancipated post-war woman he was "the symbol of everything wild and wonderful and illicit in nature" (*Life*, January 15th, 1950). He offered a dream of escape from the safe and dull life of all the Will Kennicotts of America, an eroticism which was certainly not offered by Doug, who seemed to be all the time doing all the things that adolescent boys are recommended to do to take their minds off sex.

It seemed almost incidental that Valentino had the specific qualities of a considerable screen performer. A sincerity and lack of humour gave his performances an intensity that more inhibited Anglo-Saxons rarely achieved. His early career as a ballroom dancer gave his movement a grace and rhythmic sense that — under directors of the quality of Ingram (*The Four Horsemen of the Apocalypse*) and Clarence Brown (*The Eagle*) — were communicated to the films in which he played. In the latter film and *Monsieur Beaucaire*, despite his lack of humour in certain private respects, he showed a charming feeling for light comedy.

Above all he was supremely photogenic, with his fine skin, his regular features, his sleek black hair, his deep melancholy eyes whose myopia gave them a special mystery, his eyebrows quizzically drawn together.

Born in Castellaneta (Taranto), the young Rodolfo Pietro Filiberto Guglielmi failed his course at the Venice Military Academy, and trained in agriculture. Arriving in the States in 1913 he worked as a gardener, a waiter, an exhibition dancer and a taxi dancing partner until he was given a part in a dance-hall scene in a film of 1918 (allegedly a film called *Alimony*, directed by Emmett Flynn; though no film of this description is recorded by the Library of Congress Copyright office). He continued to get parts, although generally as a dago villain, until his attractions were recognised by June Mathis, and he was cast in *The Four Horsemen of the Apocalypse* (1921). Despite his immediate success with the public, his career was uneven, largely due to difficulties with producers caused by the interference of his ambitious wife, Natacha Rambova (the adopted daughter of Richard Hudnut) and Valentino's own wild improvidence.

Valentino died very soon after finishing *The Son of the Sheik*—alone, spent, getting a little plump, heartbroken at newspaper attacks upon his "degenerating influence" upon American manhood. The posthumous success of his films enriched his estate. His death was the signal for extravagant mourning and various suicides by inconsolable female fans.

Inevitably after Valentino's appearance there was a vogue for Latin Lovers. The star's own brother Alberto (Albert Valentino) had no success with a couple of films he made for a firm called F.B.O. Productions in 1928-9. **Ramon Novarro** came nearest to duplicating Valentino's success, though his less virile beauty tended to inspire maternal rather than erotic responses. He had already appeared in one or two films when Ingram used him in *The Prisoner of Zenda*. Subsequently acquired by Metro as their reply to Paramount's Valentino, he went on to his biggest successes in *Scaramouche* (1923), *Ben Hur* (1926) and Lubitsch's *The Student Prince* (1928).

The career of **Antonio Moreno**, an ex-stage actor of Spanish birth who had been working in films since 1912, achieving his principal successes in serials, took a distinct lift in the early Twenties in the wake of the Valentino craze. He played opposite Negri in *The Spanish Dancer* (1923), Alice Terry in *Mare Nostrum* (1926) and Garbo in *The Temptress*. It was due to Moreno that Stiller was sacked from this last film: Stiller had asked him to remove the moustache which, he said (with more reason than discretion), made Moreno look like an Italian waiter. Less probably Moreno played Cyrus Waltham, the store proprietor in *It*, thus lending a touch of Latin romance to Elinor Glyn's romantic comedy. **Rod La Rocque** was born in Chicago and raised as a child actor. Brought to Hollywood by Goldwyn in 1918 he enjoyed his principal successes in DeMille's social comedies. **Ricardo Cortez** (born Jacob Krantz in Vienna, in 1899) had Valentinoesque good looks, on the strength of which, presumably, he began his Hollywood career in 1923. One feels that his career was handicapped from the start by the attempt to model him too closely on Valentino. The natural and unpretentious charm he displays in *The Pony Express*, for instance, was rarely exploited, though in later years he became a valuable character actor, and in 1939-40 directed several films.

JOHN GILBERT, born John Pringle, in Logan, Utah, was the son of the principal comic of the Pringle Stock Company. Despite these solidly native American origins, he owed his enormous success to the vogue for Latin lovers, a vogue which his fine physique and dark good looks, his piercing gaze and sudden, bewitching smile admirably suited. He had spent several years with Ince, writing as well as acting, when he was given the leading role in Emmett J. Flynn's *Monte Cristo* (1922). Gilbert's roistering private life often obscured his real seriousness as an actor. Resisting typing, his versatility is demonstrated in roles as varied as the American boy in *The Big Parade*, Lillian Gish's Rodolpho in *La Bohème* and the vicious Danilo in Stroheim's *The Merry Widow*. As Gilbert outgrew the Latin lover type to become the ardent romantic lover of the films he made with Garbo (with whom his name was romantically associated) he to an extent restored to American men the self-confidence that had been lost in this phase of idolatry, preparing

The versatile Gloria Swanson as the fool kitchen help in Allan Dwan's STAGE STRUCK (1925).

Above, an actress of great interior power, Louise Brooks, whom Hollywood condemned to a series of undistinguished flapper roles.

Right, Elinor Glyn's romantic comedy, IT (1927), directed by Clarence Badger, established the lasting legend of Clara Bow, seen here with Antonio Moreno who brought a touch of Latin romance to the film.

The spirited comedienne Marion Davies and the noted character actress Marie Dressler in King Vidor's THE PATSY (1928) with Jane Winton (left) and Del Henderson.

Nazimova, an actress of balletic grace, as Camille and the supremely photogenic idol Rudolph Valentino as Armand in Ray C. Smallwood's 1921 version of CAMILLE.

Top, Pola Negri, the image of the exotic vamp, in Mauritz Stiller's HOTEL IMPERIAL (1926). Below, an ageless and timeless beauty: Garbo in Clarence Brown's A WOMAN OF AFFAIRS (1928).

Al Jolson singing and speaking a few words: Alan Crosland's THE JAZZ SINGER (1926).

Mary Eaton in Millard Webb's GLORIFYING THE AMERICAN GIRL (1929) (the original U.S. title).

the way for the era of all-American erotic virility, represented by Clark Gable and Gary Cooper.

Of all the Latin heroes, **Gilbert Roland** (born in Mexico in 1905) might have been the best successor to Valentino; but he seemed never to get roles suited to his talents. Perhaps he arrived too late in the vogue, and miscalculated in changing his name from the more colourful Luis Antonio Damaso de Alonso. Whatever the reason, the success of this attractive actor was limited in the silent period.

Rex Ingram perceived that the real piquancy of the Latin lover was when he was seen in erotic opposition to a cool-blooded Anglo-Saxon girl, for preference the poised and elegant Alice Terry. Nevertheless the Twenties produced a school of exotic leading ladies to parallel the men. **Theda Bara**'s star had set before this. The former Theodosia Goodman of Cincinnati appeared in three films in 1918, but except for an unsuccessful attempt at a comeback in 1925 (*The Unchastened Woman*) Bara vanished definitively from the screen. Nor can Alla Nazimova quite be reckoned in this class. Since she settled in New York in 1905 she had become an American institution. Her extraordinary looks and her balletic grace were rare gifts to the cinema; but she was more inclined to classic roles — *Camille* (1921), in which she had Valentino for her Armand, *A Doll's House* (1922) and *Salome* (1923) — than the E. M. Hull class of romanticism. The Polish actress **Pola Negri** despite her equally serious theatrical background (in Warsaw and Reinhardt's *Sumurun*), better fitted the Hollywood image of the exotic vamp; and her undoubted talent (especially in Stiller's *Hotel Imperial* and in her films with Lubitsch) taken with her colourful private life (she married successively a Baron, a Count and a Prince, had a rumoured romantic liaison with Chaplin and wore widow's weeds at Valentino's funeral) endeared her to the public.

Vilma Banky came from Hungary via the Austrian cinema, to be the leading lady of two of Valentino's films, *The Eagle* (1925) and *Son of the Sheik* (1926). After Valentino's death she played in a number of films with Ronald Colman. Another of Valentino's leading ladies, the stage actress **Nita Naldi**, who appeared with him in *Blood and Sand* (1922),

A Sainted Devil (1924) and *Cobra* (1925), earned for a brief period the enviable title of "Queen of the Vampires".

There were home-grown lady exotics too. The star of *The Three Musketeers* and *The Prisoner of Zenda*, **Barbara La Marr** was in fact a girl from Richmond, Virginia, called Rheatha Watson. Her voluptuous feline beauty, before it assigned her to exotic vamp roles, had often got her into trouble. Even before her brief career began she had been raped twice, married once and been deceived by a would-be bigamist. After a whirlwind career and further complications to her private life, she died in 1926, aged 28.

Towards the end of the silent period two Mexican actresses came into prominence. **Lupe Velez** brought a striking new approach to exoticism. She was vital instead of sultry, tempestuous instead of sinister and vampiric. **Dolores Del Rio** was brought to Hollywood by First National, and by 1927 had achieved — in films like *The Loves of Carmen* (1927) and *Resurrection* (1927) — a popularity which for a brief period rivalled Garbo's.

An altogether different type of exotic sexuality was suggested by Stroheim in the roles of callously sadistic European lovers he created in his own films in the early Twenties; and by **Sessue Hayakawa**, whose career as a sinister Oriental charmer, initiated in Ince's *Wrath of the Gods* (1914) but pursued more significantly in DeMille's *The Cheat* (1915), continued until 1923 when he left Hollywood for Europe, and subsequently Japan.

The hunger for heroes could take in other varieties of eccentric. **Marie Dressler**, a stage actress who had worked briefly in the cinema during the war, making various comedies based on her stage success *Tillie's Nightmare*, returned to Hollywood in 1927 to begin a career as a character actress, which reached its peak in the early Thirties. In *The Callaghans and the Murphys* (1927) she was cast opposite Polly Moran, who subsequently frequently partnered Dressler. **Louise Dresser** abandoned a successful stage career at the age of forty to work in films. Of her silent performances the alcoholic ex-prima donna in *The Goose Woman* and Catherine the Great in *The Eagle* are best remembered.

(The latter performance provides an interesting comparison with her subsequent role as the Czarina Elisabeth in Sternberg's *The Scarlet Empress.*) **Wallace Beery** entered the cinema in 1912, two years after his brother Noah and after a career in circus and musical comedy. In the Twenties he established himself as a favourite heavy, though as the decade wore on his essentially comic outlook asserted itself more and more, to establish him firmly as the sort of lovable rogue he plays in *The Pony Express* and in his later sound films. **George Bancroft**, the villain in *The Pony Express* and Sternberg's favourite gangster (*Underworld, The Docks of New York*) was a similar case in which a natural warmth and affection were belied by a tough and brutally powerful appearance.

The search for idols seems unlimited. There were the child stars who followed in the wake of **Jackie Coogan**'s triumphant career. After *The Kid* (1921, when he was seven) he starred in more than a dozen silent films, gave an audience to the Pope, and made a fortune (which was squandered in subsequent lawsuits to wrest the money from the hands of his mother and stepfather). His contemporaries included Baby Peggy (retired 1923, aged 5), Mitzie Green, and Baby Madge who retired in 1920 at the age of eleven but made a comeback later as Madge Evans. From 1922 there was a whole school of Hal Roach *Our Gang* stars.

Even animals achieved stardom. Apart from Hal Roach's zoological equivalent of *Our Gang*, the Dippy-Doo-Dads Comedies which were played entirely by animals, there were such individual stars as Teddy, the comic dog on the Keystone lot, Brownie, Century Comedies' dog artist and — king of them all — Rin-Tin-Tin (*c.*1917-1932) who made more than forty films, earned 1,500 dollars a week in his prime, and was cited by his trainer's wife as sufficient cause for divorce. He really was a wonder dog. The tricks he performs without benefit of cutting devices are still incredible. In *Clash of the Wolves* (1925) he reveals a comic side to his nature as well, solemnly playing one sequence in bootees and a set of false whiskers. Several horses, equally, achieved fame in Westerns: W. S. Hart's Midnight and Fritz (who plays the title role in *Pinto Ben*), Ken Maynard's Tarzan, and so on.

The comedians were a class of their own, deserving separate consideration. The comic strip caricatures of the Sennett era slapsticks — the fat men, the thin men, the whiskery men, the fat ladies, slobby Arbuckle, cross-eyed and bird-like Ben Turpin, pickle-faced Ford Sterling, myopic Chester Conklin, gigantic Mack Swain, Larry Semon the mad pierrot, gave place to altogether more sophisticated concepts of character comedians, as clowns began to follow the general movement of the cinema to feature-length films. The comedians of the silent cinema, wrote James Agee, "simplified and invented, finding out new and much deeper uses for the idiom. They learned to show emotion through it, and comic psychology, more eloquently than most language has ever managed to, and they discovered beauties of comic motion which are hopelessly beyond reach of words."

Keaton, Chaplin, Harold Lloyd, Laurel and Hardy have already been discussed in Chapters 5, 6 and 7; and the reader is referred for a more extended treatment of Hollywood's great comic stars to "4 Great Comedians", by Donald W. McCaffrey (Zwemmer/Barnes 1968).

★ ★ ★

As the silent period approached its close, however, all the stars — flappers, dogs, vamps, babies, clowns and Latin lovers — were eclipsed. The story of how Mayer had brought to Hollywood a tall, strange, shy, awkward Swedish girl, along with Mauritz Stiller — whose role in transforming a jolly shop-girl into the greatest and most melancholy actress in the world was that of a modern Svengali — is legend (see Chapter 4). The art, too, of **GRETA GARBO** is legend — inexplicable and beyond analysis. She possessed a rare photogenic quality. Ungainly, big-limbed, hollow chested, she seemed nevertheless to be the most graceful creature who ever moved. The most uncomely of fashions in hair and clothes could never disguise her ageless and timeless beauty.

As an actress she never made a move or (when talkies came) delivered a line which seemed false or miscalculated. She worked with good directors and bad ones, was happy with some and miserable with others. But none of them ever really affected her extraordinary, radiant, indefinable talent. With Garbo you were aware less of an actress than of a soul exposed to life and to mankind. The depth and intensity of her acting — which was rather, being — metamorphosed anything she played. She made ten silent films in Hollywood: if they were not novelette rubbish to begin with (and there is nothing very wrong with *Anna Karenina*) they ended up that way after the Metro script department had done their stuff and Mayer and Thalberg had said their separate says. But Garbo gave them a little of her own divinity.

The public recognised her stature perhaps before the studio; and deifying her, turned indifferent to most of its old loves. The Thirties were to bring new idols and new fashions in idols; but for the moment the advent of Garbo provided a watershed in Hollywood idolatry.

9. The Crack-Up

IN THIRTY YEARS a totally new art had developed, whose apogee can be glimpsed in works like *Strike*, *The Wedding March*, *Way Down East*, *The General*, *The Master of the House*, *The Iron Horse*, *The Wind*; in the playing of Chaplin, Gish, Garbo, Stroheim, Barthelmess, Mosjoukin, Jannings, Keaton, and Veidt. The cinema of the years between 1918 and 1928 presents a record which would be astonishing in any art form. And suddenly, as the post-war decade neared its end, this art which had developed its own techniques and language was rendered anachronistic and defunct. Never before had an art form been cut off so completely. Richard Griffith speaks movingly of the loss the cinéastes and intellectuals of the time felt: "Whatever improvements it might have developed if it had survived a few years longer, the silent film at its best had by 1928 attained singular completeness as a human experience. To walk into a darkened theatre, to focus upon a bright rectangle of moving light, to listen somewhat below the level of consciousness to music which was no longer good or bad in itself but merely in relation to what was on the screen, and above all to watch, in a kind of charmed, hypnotic trance a pattern of images which appeared and disappeared as capriciously as those pictures which involuntarily present themselves to the mind as it is dropping off to sleep — but which, also like those of the mind, gradually mount to a meaning of their own — this was an experience complete and unique, radically unlike that provided by the older arts or by the other new media of mass communication. It bade fair to become the characteristic art-experience of our time." (This essay, the introduction to the third part of Rotha's *The Film Till Now*, remains a classic assessment of the place of the author in the commercial cinema, of the distinction between the industrial realities of the production of a popular art and "aesthetic" evaluations of cinema artists.)

For many years sound had seemed imminent and yet remote. Experiments with synchronised sound had been familiar for years. Edison's first interest in the motion picture was as an accompaniment to his phonograph. Gaumont had synchronised gramophone records to film as early as the first years of the century. Griffith's *Dream Street* (1921) was only one of a number of films shown in the early Twenties with experimental sound sequences.

But right into the Twenties there was the lack of an amplification system adequate to the huge picture palaces that were in vogue after the war. Moreover the prospect of a large-scale changeover to sound was hardly attractive to producers whose stages and costly equipment would be rendered obsolete; to theatre owners who equally would need to re-equip their houses; to actors, who were naturally alarmed at the prospect of having to learn new techniques and to expose themselves to new demands; to film-makers, who had developed a highly sophisticated medium which they were understandably unwilling to abandon. And the public for the moment seemed happy enough with the entertainment they had (though this might have been an illusion. Reliable statistics are hard to come by; but there are signs that the audience may have reached a peak in the early Twenties and that attendances were beginning to suffer from a certain boredom with the standardised monotony of the bulk of the studios' immense output).

The portents were not entirely ignored, however. William Fox had bought interests in two sound systems, Tri-Ergon and Case, quite early in the period. Meanwhile the Warner Brothers, somewhat left behind in the race to gain control of the exhibition end of the industry, were fighting for survival. In the middle of the craze for mergers, not even Cohn's Columbia Pictures, struggling up from Poverty Row, would consider a tie-up with the older firm.

Still Warners managed to get financial backing from the finance house of Goldman, Sachs. They built a million and a half dollar Hollywood movie palace, and the Broadway Warner, and purchased the old Vitagraph Company, which carried with it the tag-end of a useful contract with Famous Players-Lasky. Thereupon they gambled with sound, agreeing with Western Electric to introduce sound pictures in exchange for a royalty on every Western Electric sound instrument sold. In 1926 they presented their first Vitaphone programme, consisting of Alan Crosland's *Don Juan* and a selection of synchronised shorts of Anna Case, Mischa Elman, Martinelli *et al*, all introduced by a drab little speech from the screen by Will Hays. The Warners quickly followed up their advantage. *The Jazz Singer* had Al Jolson singing and speaking, ad lib, a few words. The *Singing Fool* contained substantial talking sequences. *The Lights of New York* introduced the all-talking film — and all-talking was no exaggeration, for the dialogue was non-stop so that the audience should not for a moment feel cheated of the exciting new screen experience.

The public responded enthusiastically; the Warners put away a trust fund for themselves of three million dollars; the rest of the industry was obliged to follow them into talking pictures. The politics of the competing systems which achieved the backing of the different industry giants was an elaborate jockeying which only ended with an international agreement on standardisation of equipment in July 1930. The introduction of sound brought about a complete revolution in the industry, and drastic power re-alignments. But the public, gratefully and innocently, was hooked; and it was probably in part due to the revived enthusiasm for the cinema brought about by sound (as well as the cinema's proven value as an opiate for depressed societies) that carried the cinema industry safely through the stock market crash and the years that followed.

★ ★ ★

The immediate effect upon the artistic quality of the Hollywood film was disastrous. Sound equipment was clumsy (cameras had to be enclosed in great sound-proof booths); and sound technique was elementary, so that camera movement was for a time practically annihilated, while editing was minimised. This, added to the need to keep actors anchored within the range of hidden microphones gave the early talking pictures a static quality which is nowadays soporific.

Cinéastes were divided between excitement at the potential of the new dimension added to the film's means, and terror. Pudovkin considered that ". . . the sound film is a new medium which can be used in entirely new ways. Sounds and human speech should be used by the director not as a literal accompaniment, but to amplify and enrich the visual image on the screen. Under such conditions could the sound film become a new form of art whose future development has no predictable limits." Eisenstein, Pudovkin and Alexandrov published a joint manifesto on the use of sound, in which they welcomed it with enthusiasm, whilst trying to work out theoretical bases for its positive use. In England, Paul Rotha, writing in 1929-30 ("The Film Till Now") considered that the dialogue film had no future, but would "pass as soon as its showmanship possibilities become exhausted." The value of synchronised sound was only valuable, he felt (along with many others of the time), as a means of recording musical accompaniments, or to reproduce the sound of objects, as against speech. Dialogue, he felt, impaired the visual power of the cinema. "It may be concluded that a film in which the speech and sound effects are perfectly synchronised and coincide with their visual images on the screen is absolutely contrary to the aim of the cinema. It is a degenerate and misguided attempt to destroy the real use of the film and cannot be accepted as coming within the true boundaries of the cinema. Not only are dialogue films wasting the time of intelligent directors, but they are harmful and detrimental to the culture of the public. The sole aim of their producers is financial gain, and for this reason they are to be resented. Any individual criticism that may be made of them may be considered as having no connection with the natural course of the film. This, as will be seen, lies in the plastic moulding of sound and visual images."

After the immediate change-over period of desperate attempts to salvage silent films already on the shelves by tacking on to them synchronised scores and talking sequences, however irrelevant, the producers' first reaction was to bring Broadway to Hollywood. Scenarists had not yet adapted themselves to the problems of the new medium, and plays were transferred word for word and scene for scene to the cinema. The bulk of stage players rushed to Hollywood proved unadaptable to the more intimate medium of the film, though a whole new generation of Hollywood actors, including people like Edward G. Robinson, Fredric March, Paul Muni and James Cagney, gradually came into being. The old Hollywood generation found the adjustment no easier. Some giants like Pickford and Fairbanks were never able to regain the momentum which their careers had had before the change-over. Other artists like Norma Shearer, Ronald Colman and Janet Gaynor found their careers taking a promising new turn. Sometimes one suspects that company politicians found the excuse that personalities or voices were unsuitable for sound films a useful excuse to rid themselves of artists of whom they were tired. John Gilbert is the example most often quoted of a star who was unable to make the transition; yet his perfectly satisfactory talking picture performances do not seem an altogether adequate explanation for the decline of his career in the early Thirties. Other artists proceeded with diplomatic caution. Chaplin waited until 1941 before risking a full-scale talking picture; *City Lights* (1931) and *Modern Times* (1936) are really silent films with a greater or less degree of synchronised musical and sound effects. Garbo rode the storm triumphant and unmoved.

It was evident that the talking picture was going to shape the Hollywood cinema into new patterns. Certain staple genres began to disappear. The silent slapstick comedy was hit hard: the technical flexibility of the silent film, the freedom to improvise and to revise the finished film in accordance with audience reactions, was lost. Great figures like Langdon and Keaton (a victim of politics rather than the revolution) disappeared from view. Other styles of comedy came to the fore, however: Laurel and Hardy made the change triumphantly; Mae West and W. C. Fields soon settled in Hollywood; the Marx Brothers introduced a whole new comic language. Other new genres flourished. Walt Disney's *Silly Symphonies* showed the way to creative uses of sound. With *Broadway Melody* a new kind of film that could only belong to the era of sound was inaugurated. The gangster film came to vivid life when audiences could hear new speech idioms as well as seeing on the screen representations of the thrilling new underworld of the Twenties.

As the Twenties came to their close, artists rose to the challenge of the new medium. The resourceful Rouben Mamoulian, brought to Hollywood in the rush of theatre people, proved himself fundamentally a cinema artist. He put the whole camera booth on wheels to restore the mobility of the camera. In *Applause* (1929; made in Paramount's New York Studios) he used two cameras and introduced the superimposition of sound tracks. In *City Streets* (1930) he used sound non-realistically — as a soliloquy, heard over a close-up of Sylvia Sidney's face, and as an impressionistic montage of aural impressions. In *Hallelujah!* Vidor showed that sound and dialogue and songs could be used for dramatic effects no less potent than he had achieved with images in *The Big Parade* and *The Crowd.* Ernst Lubitsch was delighted with the new medium and demonstrated its distinctive properties when he remade *Marriage Circle* as *One Hour With You* (1932). The early Thirties were to see Hollywood's film-makers extended as never before by the challenges of the new dimension of sound.

Index *(to films of the period and personalities; major film references in bold type)*